Reading, Research, and Writing:

Teaching Information Literacy with Process-Based Research Assignments

D1570117

By Mary Snyder Broussard

Association of College and Research Libraries
A division of the American Library Association
Chicago, Illinois 2017

The paper used in this publication meets the minimum requirements of American National Standard for Information Sciences–Permanence of Paper for Printed Library Materials, ANSI Z39.48-1992. ∞

Library of Congress Cataloging-in-Publication Data

Names: Broussard, Mary Snyder, author.
Title: Reading, research, and writing : teaching information literacy with
  process-based research assignments / by Mary Snyder Broussard.
Description: Chicago : Association of College and Research Libraries, a
  division of the American Library Association, 2017. | Includes
  bibliographical references.
Identifiers: LCCN 2017000371 (print) | LCCN 2017016346 (ebook) | ISBN
  9780838988763 (pdf) | ISBN 9780838988756 (paperback : alk. paper)
Subjects: LCSH: Information literacy--Study and teaching (Higher) | English
  language--Rhetoric--Study and teaching (Higher) | Academic writing--Study
  and teaching (Higher) | Reading (Higher education) |
  Research--Methodology--Study and teaching (Higher) | Academic
  libraries--Relations with faculty and curriculum.
Classification: LCC ZA3075 (ebook) | LCC ZA3075 .B757 2017 (print) | DDC
  001.4071/1--dc23
LC record available at https://lccn.loc.gov/2017000371

Printed in the United States of America.

21 20 19 18 17 5 4 3 2 1

Table of Contents

Acknowledgments

While my name is the only one that appears on the cover of this book, there are dozens of brilliant, patient people who have greatly contributed to its creation. Gary Hafer inspired my trip down this rabbit hole two years ago and has been extremely supportive ever since. I would like to thank everyone who reviewed pieces of this book, including April Cunningham, Donna Witek, Jeremy McGinniss, Jeff Waller, Joel Burkholder, Tiffany Towns Dwiel, Carl DiNardo, Sue Beidler, and Rachel Hickoff-Cresko. Thank you to the many others who shared specialized expertise with me, including John Bean, Erin Feld, Carrie Donovan, Maria Hebert-Leiter, Shanna Wheeler, and the always generous librarians at Gettysburg College. This project was supported by a professional development grant from Lycoming College, which has provided many other types of support as well.

Finally, this book is dedicated to my dad, who often lectured me about the importance of good writing. This book is penance for having ignored him at the time.

CHAPTER 1

Why Learn about Reading and Writing?

Literacy, as Richardson, Vygotsky, and others have defined it, is not synonymous with ability to read (decode) or write (transcribe) per se. Rather it is a "goal-directed, context-specific" behavior, which means that a literate person is able to use reading and writing in a transactional sense to achieve some purpose in the world at hand.

—Flower[1]

The research paper has become so ingrained in higher education that its benefits are assumed to be self-evident. Like many academic librarians, I took its educational purpose for granted for the first eight years of my teaching career. Yet when I began asking respected colleagues why they assign research papers, I found their rationales unsatisfying because the connection between student writing and learning remained vague. Teaching faculty and librarians often lament on the lack of critical thinking demonstrated in undergraduate research papers, a sentiment that is echoed in the professional literature.[2] Educators frequently discuss students' failure to engage with such assignments, but the more I explored the literature, the more I began to question whether we truly provide the kind of support students need in order to succeed. It may not be that students *will not* invest in research paper assignments, but that many *cannot* with the educational support we currently provide.

One of the primary functions of the academic library is to support various research assignments across undergraduates' college careers. Information literacy, the assumed domain of librarians, fits within a broader literacy. The Association of College and Research Libraries' *Framework for Information Literacy for Higher Education* (which will henceforth be

1

referred to simply as "ACRL" and "the *Framework*") defines information literacy as "the set of integrated abilities encompassing the reflective discovery of information, the understanding of how information is produced and valued, and the use of information in creating new knowledge and participating ethically in communities of learning."[3] The "reflective discovery of information" implies reading for comprehension, and "creating new knowledge" means that educators must do all they can to help students move from *knowledge telling* to *knowledge transforming* when students write research papers.[4]

Cowan argues that information literacy is nothing more than a combination of reading, writing, and critical thinking.[5] To many librarians, this may seem overly simplistic, but it is not. Rather, educators' understanding of the activities of reading and writing tend to be oversimplified, which hinders their ability to teach critical thinking in the context of research assignments. While this book strongly argues that students need additional support in reading and writing in order to develop strong information literacy skills, it does not necessarily argue that librarians should be responsible for directly teaching these subjects. However, how they teach information literacy, how they work with faculty, and how they relate to students at the reference desk should take this rhetorical and process-based approach to information literacy into consideration. Reconsidering information literacy as situated within reading and writing has the potential to make information literacy instruction much more meaningful and integrated into students' learning processes. Through the exploration of theories and research in the fields of composition, rhetoric, education, and cognitive psychology, my own perceptions of the difficulties of research papers have been replaced with a much deeper understanding of how difficult these assignments actually are.

Why Are Reading and Writing So Hard?

Reading and writing are two of the most demanding cognitive tasks that humans undertake. Their complexity masks itself in such a way that educators often do not realize how much scaffolding students need to complete them.[6] Brent says that educators tend to focus their instruction on the beginning and end of the research paper process, with little support in between.[7] Without frequent interaction with educators during the research process, most students cannot move from novice readers and writers to expert ones. The educational benefits of the research paper are indeed great, but in order to help students attain the kind of learning intended in such assignments, educators need to better understand the processes of reading and writing to create an environment more conducive to learning. This section is meant to give a very broad overview and introduction to the complexities of reading and writing, and each topic will be explored in greater depth in the chapters that follow. If educators ignore these complexities of reading and writing, they will be unlikely to provide the kind of support that is necessary for students to realize the educational potential of a research assignment.

One of the primary problems students must overcome is the notion that good writing comes only from naturally gifted writers. Writers are often depicted in mass media as sitting down at a computer (or a typewriter in older movies) and dashing off a novel over a very short period of time. Furthermore, many educators have reached a level of expertise over time so that they can function at very high levels in reading, writing, and disciplinary thinking without realizing how difficult the literacy activities in which they engage actually are. The cognitively and emotionally demanding work that leads to good writing is hidden from the reader and is often easily forgotten by the writer. Educators can greatly assist students by teaching writing as a messy, iterative process and by developing assignments that encourage process-based research practices.

In his seminal book *The Psychology of Writing*, Kellogg sheds light on why writing is so difficult. He describes thoughts as "personal symbols"; they can be events, mental images, associations, emotions, or words.[8] Verbal language, whether written or spoken, is a learned set of "consensual symbols." In order to communicate with others, writers or speakers must translate personal symbols into consensual symbols to convey information. Readers or listeners must then convert the consensual symbols into their own personal symbols to understand the information being conveyed. Communication, therefore, happens through symbolic negotiation between the writer/speaker and the reader/listener, which does not happen automatically for either party. It takes a great deal of cognitive effort to communicate through language. Experienced readers and writers have developed strategies for dealing with these difficulties, but usually undergraduates have yet to learn such strategies, which is particularly evident when reading their research papers.

This conversion cycle between personal and consensual symbols is recognized as "meaning making" and is frequently discussed in the composition and reading comprehension literatures.[9] Making meaning through reading is a much more interactive and dynamic process than most educators realize. Reading is more than simply decoding the printed symbols on the page into individual words; when effective readers engage with a text, they utilize a lifetime of background knowledge, knowledge of vocabulary, and knowledge of the conventions of the text's genre in order to make meaning from it. For example, due to limited space and time, road sign creators rely heavily on drivers' previous experiences to communicate important information. Children learn the meanings of common road signs such as traffic lights and stop signs long before they learn to drive. However, less common signs that override the usual rules of traffic can be difficult to understand, such as under which circumstances one can turn left at a congested five-way intersection. Drivers are likely to be able to decode the sign—to understand what each word means—but may not be able to read the sign for comprehension and will therefore be unable to respond appropriately. Likewise, undergraduates are frequently expected to read texts for which they have no relevant background knowledge to draw from, and therefore it should be no surprise when they struggle (or fail) to respond to these texts appropriately.

These bundles of background knowledge, called *schemata* (singular *schema*), allow readers to read *beyond* the text, otherwise known as analyzing or thinking critically about a text.[10] Schemata are the mental containers or structures that help people store information in long-term memory in meaningful ways, improving the information's potential for future retrieval. They also help readers fill in the gaps of what is unknown, such as how to react to an unfamiliar road sign. As people learn new information, they compare it to relevant schemata in their previous knowledge and decide if the new information fits within what they already know or believe. If so, they incorporate the new information into the existing schemata. If not, they either change their schemata or reject—partially or entirely—the new information.[11] Additionally, the reader's own rhetorical goal, or purpose for reading, will further influence how he or she interprets a text.

Meaning making is also a significant part of the writing process. It is commonly thought (and taught) that writers use writing to simply communicate what they want to say. However, many composition and rhetoric scholars contend that writers use writing to *discover* what it is that they want to say.[12] In fact, the best *learning* through writing happens as a result of struggling to figure out what to say and how to say it.[13] In this model of writing, the writer reads, plans, writes, and revises in a messy, iterative (nonlinear) cycle. It is through revision of written drafts, when writers must literally re-see their own work, that they are inevitably forced to solidify their own schema on the topic. It is only when writers put their thoughts on paper that they are able to test how complete and logical their ideas really are.[14] Revision allows writers to reshape their meaning in order to develop complex ideas a little at a time. In formal writing that is to be shared with others, a strong sense of responsibility toward their future audiences drives mature writers to thoroughly question, develop, and resolve their own understandings during revision. As Elbow explains, "Writing helps people to step outside their language and see it as an external object. Writing can help us plan and revise and thereby figure out complex or difficult thinking."[15] Through this process, writers continue to make meaning for themselves as well as for their future readers.

Reigning over the meaning-making process for both reading and writing is metacognition, which is frequently described as "thinking about thinking." However, this definition is not functionally useful. Instead, it is better to think of metacognition in reading and writing as the awareness and ability to control the many individual skills, strategies, and decisions involved in literacy and learning. Even expert readers and writers hit roadblocks and dead ends. It is metacognition (at various levels of consciousness) that they use to analyze the problem and find a solution or work through a list of possible solutions until they can break through the blockage and proceed.[16]

One important function of metacognition involves coping with the cognitive load of reading and writing. Reading and writing place a very high demand on working memory, which is the kind of memory required for "short-term conscious thought."[17] Cognitive psychology has long emphasized the very finite limits of working memory, which can do only so much at one time. Yet as students master lower-level literacy skills, they free the cognitive resources required for higher-level tasks. For writing, this means mastering lower-level skills such as basic spelling, handwriting, or typing allow thoughts to flow onto paper or a computer screen more fluidly so that the writer can concentrate on ideas more and transcription less. For reading, this means mastering decoding and learning the vocabulary of the domain allow the reader to focus on the meaning of the text rather than individual words. Because of these limitations on working memory, it is also critical that the process of writing a research paper be broken down and drawn out over time to avoid cognitive overload. Much of the rest of this book will focus on how to help undergraduates deal with the limitations of working memory during research projects.

Despite the fact that expert readers and writers can function at high levels in both of these activities, neither is ever completely mastered. Unlike the proverbial example of riding a bike, where the basics do not require relearning, reading and writing skills require ongoing use and practice without ever reaching a state of complete mastery.[18] Everyone continues to grow as readers and writers as long as they continue to challenge themselves. Bereiter and Scardamalia explain that "writing is a task that keeps growing in complexity to match the expanding competence of the writer. Thus, as skill increases, old difficulties tend to be replaced by new ones of a higher order."[19] It is important for educators to remember that even students who are expert readers and writers in one domain may struggle and need assistance when reading or writing in a new, unfamiliar domain.

The last several pages have explored the cognitive aspects of reading and writing. However, the affective aspects are also extremely important as they relate to motivation and confidence, which are both critical to achieving quality reading and writing. The emphasis that the writing literature places on informal writing, particularly drafting, not only spreads out the cognitive load of the activity, but also has a great deal of potential to boost a writer's motivation and confidence. It is the fear of rejection and public failure that keep many people from ever writing, or many students from ever seriously trying to write well. Low-stakes writing, such as journaling or early drafts, provides writers with a safe space to experiment with and develop messy ideas and words before they construct something worth sharing.

Why Do Librarians Need to Revisit the Research on Reading and Writing?

The library and information science (LIS) literature tying information literacy to composition and rhetoric studies is generally limited to very practical descriptions of collaborations between individual librarians and composition instructors or writing centers. Only isolated articles tie the theories of the two disciplines together. However, the recent development, discussion, and adoption of the *Framework* provide a professional environment in which academic librarians are more likely than ever to radically rethink how they teach information literacy. There is a renewed emphasis on theory and pedagogy to help librarians and teaching faculty identify what they are trying to accomplish and how they will be most likely to succeed. In discussing how to go about implementing the *Framework*, Beilin strongly encourages librarians to draw on theories from disciplines outside of librarianship.[20] Because writing instruction programs share so many of the same goals and difficulties, composition and rhetoric is a logical discipline from which to borrow a teaching praxis, or practice based on theory.

Many teaching faculty have improved student learning through the Writing across the Curriculum movement, which promotes discipline-specific writing instruction outside of composition courses. Theory from the field of composition and rhetoric and Writing across the Curriculum can greatly enrich information literacy instruction and help make research paper assignments more meaningful experiences for students. This section will continue by looking at several major problems that teaching faculty and librarians currently face with the traditional research paper assignment that could be improved with theory and research from the field of composition and rhetoric. The discussion and possible solutions from the literature in these fields will be explored in future chapters.

PROBLEM 1:
Teaching Faculty and Librarians Are Not Satisfied with Student Research Papers, and Students Seem Frustrated and Unmotivated to Do the Necessary Work

How often have you heard teaching faculty criticizing students' procrastination, website-filled bibliographies, lack of source integration, and complaints that no information could be found on their topic? Brent writes that before he looked into the research on reading, his students' "papers, by and large, remained hollow imitations of research, collections of information gleaned from sources with little evaluation, synthesis, or original thought. They approached the research as they would gathering shells at the beach, picking up ideas with interesting colors or unusual shapes and putting them in a bucket without regard for overall pattern."[21]

Larson criticizes the generic "research paper" assignment in English composition classes and goes on to write, "I would argue that most undergraduate papers reflect poor or inadequate research."[22] Howard and colleagues write, "These students are not writing from sources; they are writing from sentences selected from sources."[23] In the LIS literature, Stilling discusses how librarians commonly observe numerous students selecting the easiest sources, such as those that appear on the first page of database result lists or those immediately available in full text, rather than the most appropriate sources.[24] Holliday and colleagues recently published a report in which teaching faculty and librarians analyzed nearly 900 student research papers and found that students struggled with critical thinking, evaluating and synthesizing information, and using information effectively in their writing.[25] Furthermore, many papers were poorly organized, used irrelevant details, and did not use quotations effectively. Clearly, educators are frustrated by students' research papers.

Not surprisingly, the scholarly literature encapsulates educators' frustrations and perspectives more than students'. In one of the few studies that directly captures the negative emotions of students toward the research paper, Nelson and Hayes looked at students' research logs.[26] Interestingly, the students who adopted low-investment research strategies—those who strove for efficiency and focused on finding "facts"—found the research creation process to be "extremely boring" and "dumb busy work," whereas students who adopted high-investment strategies—those who labored to develop a specific angle on a topic—found the process engaging and rewarding. While limited, this study provides some validity to the assumptions that students are frustrated, confused, and fearful of the research paper, but such feelings are not necessarily the result of laziness.

Stilling writes, "Student papers may disappoint you because you asked students to 'compare,' 'synthesize,' 'evaluate,' or 'argue'—and they did something else."[27] It feels as if students, teaching faculty, and librarians are each speaking their own language because they are. Studies such as those conducted by Schwegler and Shamoon, Flower and colleagues, and Holliday and Rogers compare how the various groups differ in interpreting research assignments.[28] Each group has its own consensual symbols (vocabulary) that members have developed within their respective communities based on common experiences. One of the most important challenges in supporting research paper assignments is to bridge this language gap between the three groups so that all stakeholders are working toward the same goal.

Despite the existence of support services such as tutoring, writing centers, and reference desks, the composition and rhetoric literature argues that students should be getting more support in the research process than they currently are. However, it can be difficult for teaching faculty and librarians to find relevant professional literature to develop in this area. While there is no shortage of literature on how to write a research paper, such sources generally focus on mechanical skills, such as how to use a library, how to create a draft, and the conventions of grammar one should use to edit a final copy. All of these focus on the final *product* more than the *process* a writer must take to get there. They provide little help in developing the critical-thinking skills students require to benefit from research paper assignments.

PROBLEM 2:
The Many Misconceptions about the Research Process Are Perpetuated by the Current System of Teaching Research and Writing as a Much Simpler Process Than It Actually Is

Many of the reasons that teaching faculty, librarians, and students are frustrated with the traditional research paper are because our education system inadvertently teaches students that research and writing are much more straightforward than they actually are. This situation exacerbates students' negative emotions when they subsequently struggle with research assignments. Such students are all the more likely to feel that they are not naturally gifted writers when writing is not as easy as they were led to believe. Hafer says that students' "nosebleed high" expectations for writing can "dissuade them from starting" if they are not also introduced to the difficult process that all writers go through to achieve great writing.[29] If students do not receive this introduction and subsequent support for the process, educators may inadvertently encourage them to surrender to their perceived lack of intelligence or writing ability.

The research on the reading and writing processes is sympathetic to students regarding their poor performance on research paper assignments. Educators tend to value mechanical correctness above all else.[30] Furthermore, students are given too few low-stakes opportunities to improve thinking and writing before they are evaluated in high-stakes assessments. In the instruction that accompanies a research paper assignment, educators do not emphasize how messy and nonlinear the reading, thinking, or drafting processes are. Even the vocabulary that educators use is evidence of their focus on the final product. Brent argues that educators should replace the term *research paper* with *writing-from-sources*, because "it changes the focus from what the product *is* to what the writer *does*."[31] This book will use this term heavily to describe a process-based approach to written research assignments.

While teaching faculty frequently mention numerous mechanical errors in their complaints on the quality of students' research papers, many of these errors can be blamed on cognitive overload.[32] Cognitive load theory states that difficult and complex tasks should be broken up into more manageable pieces in order to avoid overload.[33] Expert writers spread out the cognitive load of writing, often without being consciously aware of it. They take notes, keep research journals, make numerous drafts, and talk to colleagues, to name just a few activities. As few students have the knowledge or skills to be able to spread out the cognitive load of writing-from-sources themselves, educators could improve the probability of student success by designing devices that break up a large assignment. In addition to spreading out the cognitive load of writing-from-sources, this also discourages procrastination, provides opportunities for formative and constructive feedback, and discourages plagiarism in student writing.[34]

While many teaching faculty do break down assignments into steps such as theses, outlines, annotated bibliographies, and drafts, many of these efforts are less effective than they could be because they are not based on a thorough understanding of the writing process. For example, requiring an unchangeable thesis statement or outline early in the process does not allow students the flexibility to transform their research question into something more sophisticated as they explore the topic more deeply through reflective reading and writing. Such requirements for an early thesis frequently terminate any possibility of students transforming their knowledge. Likewise, annotated bibliographies that are only summaries of sources do not guide students through thinking about their appropriateness for the purpose and topic of their own paper or how they relate to the scholarly conversation on the topic.[35] The mini assignments that lead up to a final research paper should be designed based on what is known about the expert writing-from-sources process so that these mini assignments are not simply hoops to jump through but actually contribute to the final product.

Educators who participate in scholarly writing can struggle to teach what they themselves are good at due to the "Expertise Reversal Effect," also known as the "Expert Blind Spot."[36] Dehaene writes, "In the twenty-first century, the average person still has a better idea of how a car works than of the inner functioning of his own brain."[37] Experts are likely to have such automated metacognitive skills and problem-solving strategies and have gotten so lost in the flow of writing that, in the end, they forget how much cognitive and emotional effort was required to create the final product.[38] Learners are therefore too often left to develop critical reading and writing skills on their own. Brookfield, in discussing how to become a critically reflective teacher, says educators need to look at their own instruction through four lenses: one's autobiography as learners and teachers, students' perspective, colleagues' experiences, and the theoretical literature.[39] Indeed, it is only through a combination of all four of these lenses that educators will be able to overcome the Expert Blind Spot in order to come to understand their own expert processes and find pedagogical strategies that effectively help students become critical thinkers, readers, and writers.

PROBLEM 3:
Academic Librarians Are Struggling to Break Away from the One-Shot Model of Information Literacy Instruction

As bibliographic and information literacy instruction evolved over the second half of the twentieth century, the one-shot model became the standard for its delivery. In this model, teaching faculty bring their students to the library for a one- or perhaps two-hour guest lecture on the research skills and tools needed to complete the research assignment designed by teaching faculty. Librarians have been arguing for decades that this model is not effective.[40] Recently, the one-shot has been described as "a charade where the skilled teach the reluctant, resulting in something (as opposed to nothing) but signifying little"[41] and "an inefficient and inadequate means of prepping students to incorporate meaningful research into their writing."[42]

Wiggins and McTighe point out that no educator ever has enough time to cover all of the content he or she wants students to learn. Educators must therefore focus on the "big ideas" of their discipline.[43] These big ideas are transferrable and help connect isolated skills and concepts. The *Framework* attempts to provide academic librarians with a list of the big ideas in information literacy, to "lead learners to a more holistic understanding of the processes, possibilities, and responsibilities involved in becoming more adept in our information ecosystem: the 'why,' not just the 'how.'"[44] The *Framework* calls for much higher levels of student performance in the areas of evaluation, understanding the nature of scholarly discourse, and creation of new knowledge than ACRL's *Information Literacy Competency Standards for Higher Education* did.[45]

Gibson and Jacobson, the cochairs of the task force responsible for developing the *Framework*, admit that librarians cannot teach the skills and concepts of the *Framework* in a single class period.[46] They write, "We feel it is important to provide a model that encourages conversations that explore other options. Librarians might collaborate with faculty members to flip the classroom, for example, or instructors might build information literacy instruction into course content, or departments might address how their majors will become proficient in the information-related aspects of that field."[47] Clearly, the *Framework* discourages the continuation of the one-shot information literacy instruction model, leaving instruction librarians in a difficult position.

Many librarians already realize the solution to the problems created with teaching information literacy in one-shot sessions involves collaboration with teaching faculty, which is frequently discussed in the LIS literature, but these collaborations remain problematic. Such relationships can be unequal, shallow, or dependent on individual faculty members who may leave the institution, or the collaborators may not agree on goals and priorities. Informed on the pedagogy of writing-from-sources, librarians will be in a stronger position to collaborate with teaching faculty to improve student learning and performance on writing-from-sources assignments. They can initially teach topics such as (but not limited to) reading comprehension strategies or information synthesis, then rely on the teaching faculty to provide the opportunities for extended practice. They can work with teaching faculty to design writing-from-sources assignments that better align with what is known about making such assignments effective learning experiences. Finally, they can consult and advocate with faculty to teach information literacy without direct contact with students. Information literacy, under any name, is too large and important a learning outcome in higher education to be left to guest lectures, particularly when the one-shot model is well known to be so ineffective. Adopting a rhetorical, process-based approach to information literacy and reducing artificial barriers created by interdepartmental politics have infinite potential for improving students' writing-from-sources processes and products and the knowledge they gain through the experience.

PROBLEM 4:
Academic Librarians Frequently Talk about Lifelong Learning, Which Implies Transfer, Yet There Is Little to No Evidence That Students Are Able to Transfer Information Literacy Skills to Other Assignments, Other Classes, or Contexts outside of Academia

Many authors in the LIS literature freely use the words *transfer* and *lifelong learning* as an argument for the importance of teaching information literacy. That students *do* transfer the information literacy skills they learn from academic librarians seems to be broadly assumed despite anecdotal evidence to the contrary. Yet almost no studies exist within the profession on *if* or *how* information literacy skills transfer from one context to another, and the few that do exist are primarily limited to those that survey freshmen about their incoming knowledge and skills.[48] Lloyd's study looked at the transfer of college graduates' information literacy skills to their professional lives, and she found no evidence of transfer.[49]

The concept of learning transfer became more prominent when the final draft of the *Framework* was released with the addition of "big ideas" to the document's theoretical underpinnings. As was recently alluded to in Problem 3, Wiggins and McTighe introduce the concept of big ideas in disciplines as a way for educators to prioritize the massive amounts of information they want to impart to students by focusing on the parts of a discipline that are central to understanding that discipline. These authors repeatedly state that one of the primary qualities of a big idea is that it is transferable.[50] Because transfer is now such an important part of the theoretical underpinnings of the *Framework*, and because the term *information literacy* has implied teaching an independent ability to learn for decades, it deserves a special discussion.

Kuglitsch wrote an important article entitled "Teaching for Transfer: Reconciling the *Framework* with Disciplinary Information Literacy," in which she also criticized the lack of studies in the LIS literature on information literacy and transfer.[51] She said that focusing on transfer has the potential to solve several problems information literacy programs currently face, including students viewing their multiple information literacy sessions as repetitive. She speculated that through reflection assignments in an information literacy program designed for transfer, students will recognize how they can incorporate these skills into different disciplines or apply information literacy skills in increasing complexity as they advance in their major. While Kuglitsch's article begins to fill in the scholarship gap on information literacy and knowledge transfer, LIS scholars should continue to conduct research in this area.

Librarians can begin to fill the gap in the research on transfer of information literacy skills by looking at what researchers know about facilitating the transfer of reading and writing skills. This body of literature is quite considerable, as one of the primary goals of composition instructors and the Writing across the Curriculum movement is to create graduates who are independent writers. The literature states that everyone continues to develop as readers and writers throughout their lives.[52] As their skills progress, they move on to higher-order challenges. While expert readers and writers can do this on their own, novice ones need guidance as they develop the necessary skills to gradually become more independent. Drawing on learning transfer theories in the field of rhetoric and composition, librarians can increase the likelihood of transfer of information literacy skills through the promotion of metacognition (developed through reflection), generative dispositions, problem-solving strategies, and helping students draw on the knowledge and skills they already possess through cuing.[53] Suggestions for how librarians can do this will be shared throughout this book.

This Book

The LIS literature is full of descriptions of how information literacy instruction, as currently practiced, does not achieve the learning outcomes librarians desire. Given the well-documented frustrations with the perceived lack of motivation, critical thinking, and product quality students demonstrate in their research assignments, it is clearly a good time to rethink our approach to information literacy. Yet there has been no clear proposal for an inclusive rhetorical and process-based approach to information literacy. Composition and rhetoric scholarship has the potential to help librarians rethink what information literacy is and how to teach it.

Despite how often the LIS literature mentions students using information sources from the library to write papers, its authors have rarely drawn from the rhetoric and composition literature to enhance their own practice.[54] There have been isolated articles over the past twenty-five years that have argued for rhetorical approaches to information literacy, where information literacy is embedded in what is known about how people learn through reading and writing. The most influential articles were written by Fister and Norgaard. In 1993, Fister published an article entitled "Teaching the Rhetorical Dimensions of Research," in which she urged librarians to go beyond information retrieval and evaluation.[55] She argued that overemphasis on retrieval systems implies to students that the goal of the assignment is to collect and report on individual, decontextualized pieces of information rather than "construct[ing] a text."[56] She went on to advise readers, "Rather than describe the search process as a matter of finding information—which sounds like panning for solid nuggets of truth—librarians should describe it as a way of tapping into a scholarly communication network. In this network scholars present new ideas, argue for new interpretations of old ideas, draw connections, point out contrasts, inquire into meaning, and interpret the signifiers of cultures in ways that construct meaning. And for every claim made, evidence is marshaled for support."[57] How librarians present and talk about sources and the research process has profound effects on how students view and complete writing-from-sources assignments, a conclusion that has been reiterated by Burkholder and by Holliday and Rogers.[58]

Norgaard, a writing and rhetoric scholar, wrote a two-part article in *Reference and User Services Quarterly* a decade later, arguing that information literacy instruction could benefit from the "theoretical foundations and pedagogical frameworks that inform rhetoric and composition."[59] He contended that contemporary approaches to information literacy instruction were skills-oriented and product-focused, taught as a "lock-step sequence that focuses on selecting, narrowing, and outlining a subject."[60] In contrast, through a rhetorical view of information literacy, a research assignment can be viewed "not just… as a formalistic tool for the communication of already discovered ideas but as a vehicle for inquiry and as a process of making and mediating meaning."[61] In one of his concluding remarks, he pointed out that the stakes are too high to not recognize and act on librarians' and compositionists' shared goals for students.

This book was born from frustration and a deep feeling that something in my teaching was profoundly off. My instruction felt superficial, simplistic, and mechanical, and I began to question whether the research paper was actually an effective assignment. While over time I found articles arguing for rhetorical approaches to information literacy, such as Fister's and Norgaard's, I was disappointed to see that no one had yet tackled this topic holistically. The more I read, the more my perceptions of what information literacy is and how I should teach it began to fundamentally change.

This personal search for ways to improve my own teaching coincided with the profession's discussions about transitioning from the *Standards* to the *Framework*. Rhetorical approaches to information literacy can greatly enhance one's understanding of the *Framework*. While there is no evidence that the task force responsible for developing the *Framework* used composition and rhetoric theory to inform the *Framework*'s drafts, this theory is surprisingly compatible with the *Framework*'s six frames and its overarching priorities. Two of the most dramatic changes that the *Framework* emphasizes over previous notions of information literacy acknowledge that students need to understand scholarly communication in order to participate in scholarly discourses themselves and that this participation should be as active creators rather than passive consumers—albeit as novice scholars. These two concepts have often appeared in the composition and rhetoric literature in the past several decades, along with practical advice for how to develop these understandings and perspectives in undergraduates.

Writing across the Curriculum has gained a lot of momentum in the past few decades. As Elmborg points out, writing instruction shares a lot of the same characteristics and goals as information literacy.[62] Instructors in neither field have enough time to develop the complex skills they are expected to teach, they grapple with questions of responsibility and remediation, they have lower status than other instructors on campus, and both struggle to balance mechanics with more conceptual skills. Yet even as the Writing across the Curriculum movement has been successful in many ways, its proponents remain frustrated by the areas in which they have not achieved success. Additionally, as a librarian, I am frequently frustrated reading the composition and rhetoric literature, wondering how it is applicable to the context in which I teach information literacy. They talk about promoting good writing, but not necessarily writing-from-sources or how writing is related to learning. Furthermore, few discuss providing undergraduates with additional reading comprehension support, a need that has yet to be filled by anyone in many institutions of higher education. Librarians have an important role to play in student learning by joining the writing-in-the-disciplines movement, but we need to develop our own literature on the topic.

For teaching faculty, the most powerful argument for adopting this approach to research paper assignments is likely to be that learning to read and write like someone in the field is directly tied to developing disciplinary procedural knowledge including critical-thinking skills. Librarians can draw on the arguments compositionists have made in the Writing across the Curriculum movement to open doors for richer collaborations with teaching faculty. Carter addresses common concerns among disciplinary faculty who argue that they cannot give up time devoted to teaching content in order to teach writing.[63] In response, he argues that it is the "relationship among knowing, doing, and writing that is concealed by the disciplinary focus on conceptual knowledge. Doing is the middle term that links writing and knowing in the disciplines."[64] Both Fister and Simmons point out that librarians, who work with multiple disciplines, are in a good position to help teaching faculty bridge the gap between their disciplinary experience and students' inexperience by explicitly revealing the peculiarities of a discipline's assumptions and scholarship.[65] Some librarians may question whether they have enough disciplinary knowledge to bridge the gap, to which Elmborg argues that they do not need to "possess foundational knowledge of the discipline, [they need only to] be active in their efforts to understand the disciplines as constructed communities."[66] Fister's and Simmons's arguments, strengthened by a willingness to understand disciplinary communities, can lead to strong collaborations between librarians and teaching faculty and will in turn lead to more authentic and effective learning experiences for students when educators across departments realize how deeply their individual instructional goals align with each other.

This book will take an in-depth, interdisciplinary look at the literature in rhetoric and composition studies, reading comprehension, cognitive psychology, education theory, and library and information science to paint a picture of what academic librarians and their teaching faculty collaborators should know about reading and writing to improve undergraduate writing-from-sources assignments. The implications for such an understanding include potentially improving students' motivation to research, analyze, and synthesize information at a deeper level; improving librarians' ability to influence effective assignment design among teaching faculty; and opening new avenues of meaningful formative assessment in library instruction.

Information literacy and writing-from-sources are important skills for college graduates who leave formal education to be professionals and, hopefully, lifelong learners. Ensuring students graduate with adequate skills in these areas is the job of instruction librarians, teaching faculty, and the administration both within the library and in the institution as a whole. All parties need to share responsibility for providing students the support that decades of research from many disciplines prove students need. The *Framework* has started the necessary profession-wide conversations that lay the groundwork for a radical restructuring of what and how information literacy is taught. Librarians must examine the broader picture that their piece fits within and work across disciplines to produce truly literate—and therefore information-literate—college graduates.

Notes

1. Linda Flower, "Introduction: Studying Cognition in Context," in *Reading-to-Write: Exploring a Cognitive and Social Process* (New York: Oxford University Press, 1990), 4.
2. Wendy Holliday, Betty Dance, Erin Davis, Britt Fagerheim, Anne Hedrich, Kacy Lundstrom, and Pamela Martin, "An Information Literacy Snapshot: Authentic Assessment across the Curriculum," *College and Research Libraries* 76, no. 2 (2015): 170–87; Doug Brent, *Reading as Rhetorical Invention: Knowledge, Persuasion, and the Teaching of Research-Based Writing* (Urbana, IL: National Council of Teachers of English, 1992).
3. Association of College and Research Libraries, *Framework for Information Literacy for Higher Education* (Chicago: Association of College and Research Libraries, 2016), 3, http://www.ala.org/acrl/standards/ilframework.
4. Carl Bereiter and Marlene Scardamalia, *The Psychology of Written Composition* (Hillsdale, NJ: L. Erlbaum Associates, 1987).
5. Susanna M. Cowan, "Information Literacy: The Battle We Won That We Lost?" *portal: Libraries and the Academy* 14, no. 1 (2014): 23–32.
6. John C. Bean, *Engaging Ideas: The Professor's Guide to Integrating Writing, Critical Thinking, and Active Learning in the Classroom* (San Francisco: Jossey-Bass, 1996); Ruth Schoenbach, Cynthia Greenleaf, Christine Cziko, and Lori Hurwitz, *Reading for Understanding: A Guide to Improving Reading in Middle and High School Classrooms* (San Francisco: Jossey-Bass, 1999); Jenny Cameron, Karen Nairn, and Jane Higgins, "Demystifying Academic Writing: Reflections on Emotions, Know-How

and Academic Identity," *Journal of Geography in Higher Education* 33, no. 2 (2009): 269–84; Ronald T. Kellogg and Bascom A. Raulerson, "Improving the Writing Skills of College Students," *Psychonomic Bulletin and Review* 14, no. 2 (2007): 237–42; Rolf Norgaard, "Writing Information Literacy: Contributions to a Concept," *Reference and User Services Quarterly* 43, no. 2 (2003): 124–30.

7. Brent, *Reading as Rhetorical Invention*, 105.
8. Ronald Thomas Kellogg, *The Psychology of Writing* (New York: Oxford University Press, 1994).
9. Ibid., 25
10. Richard C. Anderson, Ralph E. Reynolds, Diane L. Schallert, and Ernest T. Goetz, "Frameworks for Comprehending Discourse," *American Educational Research Journal* 14, no. 4 (1977): 367–81.
11. Brent, *Reading as Rhetorical Invention*.
12. Bereiter and Scardamalia, *The Psychology of Written Composition*; Kellogg and Raulerson, "Improving the Writing Skills of College Students."
13. Bereiter and Scardamalia, *The Psychology of Written Composition*.
14. Linda Flower, *Problem-Solving Strategies for Writing*, 4th ed. (New York: Harcourt Brace Jovanovich, 1993), 42.
15. Peter Elbow, *Vernacular Eloquence: What Speech Can Bring to Writing* (Oxford: Oxford University Press, 2012), 45.
16. Priscilla L. Griffith and Jiening Raun, "What Is Metacognition and What Should Be Its Role in Literacy Instruction?" in *Metacognition in Literacy Learning: Theory, Assessment, Instruction, and Professional Development*, ed. Susan E. Israel, Cathy Collins Block, Kathryn L. Bauserman, and Kathryn Kinnucan-Welsch (Mahwah, NJ: L. Erlbaum Associates, 2005), 3–18.
17. "Working Memory," in *Learning Theories A to Z*, ed. David C. Leonard (Westport, CT: Greenwood Press, 2002), 203.
18. Kellogg, *The Psychology of Writing*; Gary R. Hafer, *Embracing Writing: Ways to Teach Reluctant Writers in Any College Course* (San Francisco: Jossey-Bass, 2014).
19. Bereiter and Scardamalia, *The Psychology of Written Composition*, 5.
20. Ian Beilin, "Beyond the Threshold: Conformity, Resistance, and the ACRL Information Literacy Framework for Higher Education," *In the Library with the Lead Pipe*, February 25, 2015, http://www.inthelibrarywiththeleadpipe.org/2015/beyond-the-threshold-conformity-resistance-and-the-aclr-information-literacy-framework-for-higher-education.
21. Brent, *Reading as Rhetorical Invention*, xiii.
22. Richard L. Larson, "The 'Research Paper' in the Writing Course: A Non-form of Writing," *College English* 44, no. 8 (1982): 813.
23. Rebecca Moore Howard, Tricia Serviss, and Tanya K. Rodrigue, "Writing from Sources, Writing from Sentences," *Writing and Pedagogy* 2, no. 2 (2010): 187.
24. Glenn Ellen Starr Stilling, "Beyond the Research Paper: Working with Faculty to Maximize Library-Related Assignments," in *Integrating Information Literacy into the College Experience: Papers Presented at the Thirtieth LOEX Library Instruction Conference*, ed. Julia K. Nims, Randal Baier, Rita Bullard, and Eric Owen (Ann Arbor, MI: Pierian Press, 2003), 33–47.
25. Holliday et al., "An Information Literacy Snapshot."
26. Jennie Nelson and John R. Hayes, *How the Writing Context Shapes College Students'*

Strategies for Writing from Sources (Berkeley, CA: Center for the Study of Writing, Carnegie Mellon University, 1988).

27. Stilling, "Beyond the Research Paper," 35.

28. Robert A. Schwegler and Linda K. Shamoon, "The Aims and Process of the Research Paper," *College English* 44, no. 8 (1982): 817–24; Linda Flower, Victoria Stein, John Ackerman, Margaret J. Kantz, Kathleen McCormick, and Wayne C. Peck, *Reading-to-Write: Exploring a Cognitive and Social Process* (New York: Oxford University Press, 1990); Wendy Holliday and Jim Rogers, "Talking about Information Literacy: The Mediating Role of Discourse in a College Writing Classroom," *portal: Libraries and the Academy* 13, no. 3 (2013): 257–71.

29. Hafer, *Embracing Writing*, 67.

30. Ibid.

31. Douglass Brent, "The Research Paper and Why We Should Still Care," *Writing Program Administration* 37, no. 1 (2013): 38.

32. S. T. Perrault, "Cognition and Error in Student Writing," *Journal on Excellence in College Teaching* 22, no. 3 (2011): 47–73.

33. John Sweller, Paul L. Ayres, and Slava Kalyuga, *Cognitive Load Theory* (New York: Springer, 2011).

34. Janet McNeil Hurlbert, Cathleen R. Savidge, and Georgia R. Laudenslager, "Process-Based Assignments: How Promoting Information Literacy Prevents Plagiarism," *College and Undergraduate Libraries* 10, no. 1 (2003): 39–51.

35. Felicia Palsson and Carrie L. Mcdade, "Factors Affecting the Successful Implementation of a Common Assignment for First-Year Composition Information Literacy," *College and Undergraduate Libraries* 21, no. 2 (2014): 193–209.

36. Sweller, Ayres, and Kalyuga, *Cognitive Load Theory*; Mitchell J. Nathan and Anthony Petrosino, "Expert Blind Spot among Preservice Teachers," *American Educational Research Journal* 40, no. 4, (2003): 905–28.

37. Stanislas Dehaene, *Reading in the Brain: The Science and Evolution of a Human Invention* (New York: Viking, 2009), 2.

38. Flower, *Problem-Solving Strategies for Writing*; Elaine P. Maimon, Barbara F. Nodine, and Finbarr W. O'Connor, *Thinking, Reasoning, and Writing* (New York: Longman, 1989).

39. Stephen Brookfield, *Becoming a Critically Reflective Teacher* (San Francisco: Jossey-Bass, 1995).

40. Donald Barclay, "Evaluating Library Instruction: Doing the Best You Can with What You Have," *RQ* 33, no. 2 (1993): 195–202; Patrick Ragains, "Evaluation of Academic Librarians' Instructional Performance: Report of a National Survey," *Research Strategies* 15, no. 3 (1997): 169.

41. William Badke, "Ramping Up the One-Shot," *Online* 33, no. 2 (2009): 47–49.

42. Margaret Artman, Erica Frisicaro-Pawlowski, and Robert Monge, "Not Just One Shot: Extending the Dialogues about Information Literacy in Composition Classes," *Composition Studies* 38, no. 2 (2010): 98.

43. Grant P. Wiggins and Jay McTighe, *Understanding by Design* (Alexandria, VA: Association for Supervision and Curriculum Development, 2005).

44. Craig Gibson and Trudi E. Jacobson, "Informing and Extending the Draft ACRL Information Literacy Framework for Higher Education: An Overview and Avenues for Research," *College and Research Libraries* 75, no. 3 (2014): 250.

45. Association of College and Research Libraries, *Information Literacy Competency*

Standards for Higher Education (Chicago: Association of College and Research Libraries, 2000), http://www.ala.org/acrl/standards/informationliteracycompetency.

46. Gibson and Jacobson, "Informing and Extending the Draft ACRL Information Literacy Framework for Higher Education."

47. Ibid., 251.

48. Diane D. Kester, "Secondary School Library and Information Skills: Are They Transferred from High School to College?" in *School Library Reference Services in the 90s: Where We Are, Where We're Heading*, ed. Carol Truett (New York: Haworth Press, 1994), 9–17; Alison J. Head, *How Freshmen Conduct Course Research Once They Enter College*, (Project Information Literacy, December 5, 2013), http://projectinfolit.org/images/pdfs/pil_2013_freshmenstudy_fullreport.pdf.

49. Annemaree Lloyd, "Information Literacy: The Meta-competency of the Knowledge Economy? An Exploratory Paper," *Journal of Librarianship and Information Science* 35, no. 2 (2003): 87–92.

50. Wiggins and McTighe, *Understanding by Design*.

51. Rebecca Z. Kuglitsch, "Teaching for Transfer: Reconciling the *Framework* with Disciplinary Information Literacy," *portal: Libraries and the Academy* 15, no. 3 (2015): 457–70.

52. Donald Morison Murray, *A Writer Teaches Writing: A Practical Method of Teaching Composition*, 2nd ed. (Boston: Houghton Mifflin, 1985); Schoenbach et al., *Reading for Understanding*.

53. Doug Brent, "Transfer, Transformation, and Rhetorical Knowledge: Insights From Transfer Theory," *Journal of Business and Technical Communication* 25, no. 4 (2011): 396–420; Dana Lynn Driscoll and Jennifer Wells, "Beyond Knowledge and Skills: Writing Transfer and the Role of Student Dispositions," *Composition Forum* 26 (Fall 2012), http://compositionforum.com/issue/26/beyond-knowledge-skills.php; Judi Moreillon, *Coteaching Reading Comprehension Strategies in Secondary School Libraries: Maximizing Your Impact* (Chicago: American Library Association, 2012).

54. Norgaard, "Writing Information Literacy: Contributions to a Concept"; Celia Rabinowitz, "Working in a Vacuum: A Study of the Literature of Student Research and Writing," *Research Strategies* 17, no. 4 (2000): 337–46.

55. Barbara Fister, "Teaching the Rhetorical Dimensions of Research," *Research Strategies* 11, no. 4 (1993): 211–19.

56. Ibid., 212.

57. Ibid., 214–15.

58. Joel M. Burkholder, "Redefining Sources as Social Acts: Genre Theory in Information Literacy Instruction," *Library Philosophy and Practice* (2010): 1–11, http://digitalcommons.unl.edu/libphilprac/413; Holliday and Rogers, "Talking about Information Literacy."

59. Norgaard, "Writing Information Literacy: Contributions to a Concept"; Rolf Norgaard, "Writing Information Literacy in the Classroom: Pedagogical Enactments and Implications," *Reference & User Services Quarterly* 43, no. 3 (2004): 220–26. The quote is from the 2003 article, page 125.

60. Norgaard, "Writing Information Literacy: Contributions to a Concept," 127.

61. Ibid.

62. James K. Elmborg, "Information Literacy and Writing across the Curriculum: Sharing the Vision," *Reference Services Review* 31, no. 1 (2003): 68–80.

63. Michael Carter, "Ways of Knowing, Doing, and Writing in the Disciplines," *College*

Composition and Communication (2007): 385–418.

64. Ibid., 389.
65. Barbara Fister, "The Social Life of Knowledge: Faculty Epistemologies," in *Not Just Where to Click: Teaching Students How to Think about Information*, ed. Troy A. Swanson and Heather Jagman (Chicago: Association of College and Research Libraries, 2014), 87–104; Michelle Holschuh Simmons, "Librarians as Disciplinary Discourse Mediators: Using Genre Theory to Move toward Critical Information Literacy," *portal: Libraries and the Academy* 5, no. 3 (2005): 297–311.
66. Elmborg, "Information Literacy and Writing across the Curriculum," 75.

CHAPTER 2

Theoretical Foundations of Process-Based Information Literacy

with Rachel Hickoff-Cresko

> To embrace theory from other disciplines will inevitably require
> us to learn to adapt concepts and language from those fields.
> In other words, it will require the introduction of novel con-
> cepts and ideas, reflected in new vocabulary. But rather than
> be afraid of such importations, we should engage them to test
> their foundations as well as their usefulness.
>
> —*Beilin*[1]

Writing and reading are closely associated with critical thinking and deep learning, and writing-from-sources assignments can be extremely powerful educational experiences for students.[2] In order to create effective writing-from-sources assignments, however, it is necessary for educators to examine the theoretical foundations of such assignments and how theories from the disciplines of composition and rhetoric relate to widely accepted pedagogical theories. After an examination of these theories from other disciplines, this chapter will introduce a theory of process-based information literacy that is embedded in reading, writing, and inquiry.

There are few other learning activities in American higher education that require such independent learning and self-regulation among learners than writing-from-sources. Students are required to find their own information sources, make meaning from those sources, and develop a piece of writing with very little supervision and often very little feedback from educators during the process. Students must take ownership of their own learning process when writing-from-sources, and each student will have his or her own unique struggles that educators cannot address with group instruction. Instructors must assist students in developing the necessary skills to succeed through authentic assignment design, scaffolding, and reflection on writing-from-sources. All educators have room to grow in supporting students through this process. This chapter selects from education theories that promote meaning making and independent learning through a gradual release of responsibility from the instructor to the student.

Supporting students as they learn to write from sources will require educators to address both their cognitive and affective needs. The cognitive aspects of learning are often treated as quite obvious, but they are worth addressing here, as much is taken for granted or assumed regarding how students learn through reading and writing. Dewey argued that educators must also consider the affective side of learning as learning cannot happen without interest or engagement on the part of the student.[3] Motivation, an important affective aspect of writing-from-sources, has very obvious effects on the quality of students' final projects. The cognitive and affective aspects of reading and writing are closely intertwined, and therefore neither can be ignored in effective teaching.

Cognitive Needs

The cognitive aspects of learning are those that deal with the mental processes of making meaning and committing information to memory. It understandably tends to be the primary focus of many educators. What students understand and know should be frequently assessed by both teaching faculty and librarians. This includes supporting students as they independently make meaning over time during the writing-from-sources process.

Cognitive and Social Constructivism

Cognitive constructivists, such as Piaget, believe learners construct their own learning through active involvement in the learning process.[4] Learners' existing knowledge and personal background experiences are key to the learning process because they allow learners to approach the learning task in a way that will be meaningful to them as the best way to acquire the new information. Cognitive constructivism, because it is concerned with independent learning, falls on the student-centered end of the teacher-centered versus student-centered continuum. However, cognitive constructivist approaches to teaching and learning typically have an instructor as a facilitator of the learning experience: one who designs the experience and helps ensure the encounter with the content is impactful.

Social constructivists, such as Vygotsky, also believe that learning occurs through active individual involvement in the learning process but with the necessary element of social interaction to deepen and cement one's understanding.[5] Vygotsky believed learners could complete a task independently when that task was at the learner's *actual level* of development. In order for new learning to take place, guidance of a teacher or collaboration with peers is necessary. That which a learner is capable of achieving with external assistance is called the learner's *potential level* of development. The theoretical space between actual level of development and potential level of development is what Vygotsky referred to as *the zone of proximal development.*

Social constructivism, because of its dependence on collaboration for learning, falls in the middle area of the teacher-centered versus student-centered continuum. While students construct knowledge in their own minds, it is the instructor who facilitates the process by making the information meaningful and relevant and giving students the opportunities to explore and apply the new concepts and skills. In addition, the learners' interactions and discussions with their peers further their own understanding. The term *scaffolding* is often used to describe the support an instructor provides the students at the beginning of the instructional learning process for a particular concept. The scaffolds provide support to the student but are gradually removed as the student is increasingly able to apply the new ideas and skills independently.

Constructivism is very important in both teaching and performing writing-from-sources. Schema theory, which is frequently drawn upon in the literature on reading comprehension, elaborates on Piaget's idea of learners building on previous knowledge.[6] In order to make information more memorable and retrievable, the human brain is hardwired to look for patterns and connections that build relationships between individual pieces of information. These tentative bundles of seemingly related information are called *schemata* (singular *schema*). Effective learners select and apply appropriate schemata from their existing knowledge in order to evaluate and incorporate new information into their worldviews.

The intersection of constructivism and schema theory has several important implications for writing-from-sources. First of all, it helps conceptualize how one constructs knowledge gradually over time. The types of information sources used for writing-from-sources are frequently challenging to make meaning from. The reader is reading a text because the author of the text knows something the reader wishes to learn.[7] Such challenging texts will not likely be understood on the first reading. Readers will monitor their comprehension and apply problem-solving strategies to gradually overcome comprehension problems and use relevant schemata to evaluate the new information in order to decide what to assimilate and accommodate into their own writing and worldview. Their understanding of the topic will be tested and refined through drafting and revision. Therefore, meaning making in the inquiry process happens only over an extended period of time and is built on a foundation of what the students already know.

Secondly, constructivism and schema theory explain why information is so dynamic. As shall be explored further in chapter 4, the unique combination of skills and background knowledge that each individual learner brings to the information sources he or she engages with in order to write are critical to how one goes about making meaning from them. No two readers will understand the same text the exact same way. Furthermore, as a reader's schemata will have evolved if he or she revisits a previously read text, no two readings of the same text will conclude with the same interpretation.

The writing-from-sources literature stresses that meaning is made through the process of writing.[8] Good writing is spread out over drafts, as this book will explore in subsequent chapters, particularly chapters 3 and 5. In the writing-from-sources process, writers go back and forth between notes, outlines, drafts, and reading others' texts in a messy, frustrating, and iterative process in which they gradually formulate an understanding and an argument. Bean and Iyer specifically encourage librarians to use constructivist language when teaching information literacy so that students understand they are to use library sources to *formulate* an answer rather than to *find* one.[9]

Cognitive Load Theory

Cognitive load theory is equally important to understanding the gradual meaning-making process that happens through both reading and writing.

The human brain can do only so much at one time. Cognitive load theory elaborates on what this simple fact means to educators and learners, although it equally applies to experts, as all reading and writing are learning experiences.[10] Teachers, learners, readers, and writers all need to be aware of how memory works in order to make the most of it in the context of accomplishing cognitively intensive tasks such as reading, writing, and learning.

At the heart of cognitive load theory is the relationship between long-term memory and working memory. Dosher defines working memory as "the capacity to manipulate and maintain information over short periods (2–15 seconds) in order to support simple memory tasks such as remembering a telephone number, or more general cognitive tasks such as problem solving, simple reasoning, or reading. Working memory consists of several distinguishable memory capacities, together with executive functions that manage information retrieval, reactivation, and transformation."[11] Working memory manages connection-making processes that allow information to be understood, stored in long-term memory, and later retrieved.

The limitations of working memory are frequently mentioned in the composition literature. It is in working memory that a writer struggles with what to say and how to say it.[12] Perrault and Hafer both discuss how student writing errors are a direct result of cognitive overload, where the students try to do more at one time than their limited working memory will allow.[13] Kellogg and Raulerson write, "Working memory is severely taxed by the production of extended texts…. Mature writers concurrently juggle the planning of ideas, the generation of text, and the reviewing of ideas and text, placing heavy demands on executive attention."[14] They go on to explain how mastering certain writing skills frees up limited working memory resources for higher-level skills. Composition scholars and psychologists who specialize in the psychology of writing agree that educators must design assignments and coach students to draw out the writing process in order to avoid overloading working memory.

Because a writing-from-sources assignment has many complexly related parts, many of which must be completed simultaneously, it is said to have a high *intrinsic* cognitive load.[15] Such difficult tasks as finding information, making meaning from those sources, synthesizing, drafting, and revising are each inherently cognitively taxing tasks. There are many "elements that must be processed simultaneously in working memory because they are logically related."[16] One's attention is split between multiple tasks and multiple sources of information, many of which may not agree with each other. Additionally, poor assignment design can lead to high *extrinsic* cognitive load, which is a result of the manner of instruction. Sweller,

Ayres, and Kalyuga explain that intrinsic and extrinsic cognitive load are additive, meaning together they determine the overall cognitive load of an educational event.[17] "Learners may not even commence learning because the entire pool of working memory resources is needed to deal with the instructional processes used."[18] Writing-from-sources is an extremely difficult task in and of itself (intrinsic load), even for expert writers. Poor assignment design or lack of adequate instructional support leads to high levels of extrinsic cognitive load. The combination of the two can be fatal to all but the most motivated and independent learners—the ones who least need educators' interventions.

Expert readers and writers know that they need to use a variety of strategies to spread out the cognitive load of the difficult tasks they are trying to accomplish. For reading, this includes monitoring one's understanding of a text and using fix-up strategies when the cognitive load exceeds one's abilities.[19] For writing, this means spreading the cognitive load out over the drafting process, using more speech-like language to "speak to the page" in freewriting and early drafts and converting to reader-based prose only later in the writing process.[20] Additionally, part of an expert's expertise includes having an arsenal of strategies to deal with the split-attention effect inherent in summarizing many sources of information, also known as "information overload."

Students have yet to develop the metacognitive skills and strategies necessary to self-monitor their cognition and overcome the inevitable problems they will face. Effective teachers need to design instruction that does not overwhelm students' cognitive capacity. Because writing-from-sources is an educational activity that has an inherently high intrinsic cognitive load associated with it because of its high element of interactivity, educators need to have a solid understanding of how to reduce the extrinsic load as much as possible. They can reduce students' extrinsic cognitive load of writing-from-sources by designing assignments that encourage students to construct knowledge *gradually* through notes, outlines, drafts, and other forms of low-stakes and mid-stakes writing, as will be explored in the next three chapters.

Affective Needs

In addition to the cognitive theories on learning, students have affective needs that impact the learning process. Important affective aspects of learning through writing-from-sources include self-efficacy and motivation. Dewey argued that educators must spend time looking at student interest in the subject matter learned because it is through interest that students become active participants in their own learning.[21] Through interest and engagement, students care about achieving a positive outcome in the educational process. While the cognitive aspects of learning should be educators' primary concern, students will not achieve desirable results unless educators also address the affective aspects of learning that students (and all writers) experience.

Self-Efficacy

De la Luz Perez and Binkley define self-efficacy as "the belief that an individual has about himself/herself that his/her abilities will produce a desired result in a potentially demanding situation."[22] One's self-efficacy beliefs will impact one's ability to adapt or persevere when confronted with adversity.[23] Furthermore, efficacy beliefs shape what Bandura refers to as people's outcome expectations, which are the positive or negative results one expects from one's effort.[24] Because beliefs of personal efficacy are central to a person's agency, people have little incentive to put forth effort unless they believe they can produce the desired results.[25]

A person's perceived efficacy can "influence aspirations and strength of goal commitments, level of motivation and perseverance in the face of difficulties and setbacks, resilience to adversity, quality of analytic thinking, causal attributions for successes and failures, and vulnerability to stress and depression."[26] Pajares describes the far-reaching impact of one's self-efficacy beliefs by offering many examples of how they invade one's experience, from how they influence the choices people make, the directions they pursue, the amount of effort they expend on a task, and their persistence when confronting obstacles to how resilient they are when faced with adverse situations.[27] Furthermore, these beliefs in one's self-efficacy can impact the amount of stress and anxiety individuals experience as they engage in a task and the level of accomplishment they perceive.[28] The literature on self-efficacy typically discusses four sources individuals use to inform their self-efficacy perceptions: *mastery experience, vicarious experience, social persuasions,* and *somatic and emotional states.*

The most dominant source is *mastery experience,* which is influenced by a person's interpretations of his or her previous performance.[29] People "engage in tasks and activities, interpret the results of their actions, use the interpretations to develop beliefs about their capability to engage in subsequent tasks or activities, and act in concert with the beliefs created."[30] Students must have multitudes of opportunities to feel they have been successful with writing-from-sources. Some writers may need this more frequently than others, particularly those with low writing self-efficacy. Instructors can arrange for these opportunities and can explicitly discuss the accomplishments by explaining how the students' efforts relate to their end results.

The *vicarious experience* of observing others perform tasks is the second most influential source from which people form their self-efficacy beliefs.[31] If the individual lacks prior experience with a writing task or is limited in experience, models can be particularly powerful *if* the model is perceived to be similar to the observer.[32] Using examples of published texts, therefore, is not likely to help students develop self-efficacy as writers because the texts' creation process is hidden and the authors of such texts are unlike the student. Instead, helping students see each other's processes reveals how they share similar struggles and problem-solving strategies.

The *social persuasions* people receive from others are a third way self-efficacy beliefs can be developed. Bandura states this source tends to be less significant than either mastery or vicarious experience, yet it is still important to consider in an examination of the process of writing-to-learn.[33] Effective persuasions can not only improve a person's beliefs in his or her capabilities, but also ensure the projected success is attainable.[34] On the other hand, self-efficacy beliefs can be weakened or defeated by negative persuasions.[35] In the classroom, when students feel encouraged by their peers or their instructors, they are better able to overcome feelings of self-doubt and focus on success. This is further encouraged when the instructor purposefully designs the learning task for the students' abilities with the appropriate amount of challenge (i.e., not too easy or too difficult).

The fourth influence, believed to have the least powerful impact on efficacy beliefs, involves *somatic and emotional states* such as anxiety or enthusiasm.[36] Pajares states that a person's degree of confidence when confronting a task can be measured by the emotional state he or she experiences when contemplating the action.[37] This is where instructors need to focus on allowing their students to experience the joy of writing-from-sources through low-stakes opportunities for practice and promoting genuine curiosity.

Motivation

One of the biggest factors in predicting a person's success in a challenging activity is that of motivation. Dewey describes *interest* (motivation) as the force that changes one from being a passive spectator to an active participant who tries to influence the outcome in his or her favor.[38] Oka says that motivation is "the force behind behavior and provides an explanation for why people do things."[39] Without motivation, learning does not happen. Students need to feel motivation to put forth the considerable effort, take the risks, and practice the persistence that are required by writing-from-sources assignments.

Motivation is frequently described as being either extrinsic or intrinsic. Extrinsic motivation is driven by consequences, such as grades, financial gain, or approval. Intrinsic motivation is driven by enjoyment and satisfaction in the task itself, where participants find the activity "inherently valuable and satisfying."[40] In the context of writing-from-sources, intrinsic motivation can also be called *curiosity*. Passionate curiosity has the power to drive students to not only think, but think critically. It leads them to persistence through the messy process of inquiry, reading, and writing. One of the goals of educators who design and support writing-from-sources assignments is to design assignments that help students develop the intrinsic motivation to learn through writing by promoting curiosity.

Curiosity is a form of motivation that combines the affective and the cognitive aspects of learning. Fulwiler writes, "Curiosity is the necessary precondition to writing well about anything: The more questions you have, the more likely you are to pursue answers; the more answers you have, the more you have to write about."[41] Leslie describes curiosity as beginning with "an itch to explore."[42] He goes on to say that "unfettered curiosity is wonderful; unchanneled curiosity is not. When diversive curiosity is entrained—when it is transformed into a quest for knowledge and understanding—it nourishes us. This deeper, more disciplined, and effortful type of curiosity is called epistemic curiosity,"[43] which he calls "the best motivator of learning."[44]

Professional scholars are frequently driven by intense curiosity. Leist writes, "When a working academic starts a research project, that project is usually involved with some aspect of his or her professional existence which has caused the person to be disturbed in some way."[45] Bean calls this feeling of difference between what one knows and what one *wants* to know "cognitive dissonance."[46] Educators can promote curiosity in students by teaching them how to ask questions. Question asking is not an innate skill; students must be taught.[47] Educators' "goal [should be] to get students personally engaged with the kinds of questions that propel writers through the writing process."[48]

It is important to note that intrinsic motivation is directly related to a willingness to participate in more *difficult* cognitive work. Students are not motivated by easy assignments. Oka describes the qualities that lead to intrinsically motivated learners as an activity that is "optimally challenging," novel and interesting, provides a sense of control, and satisfies curiosity.[49] Writing-from-sources assignments that promote intense curiosity and are combined with the necessary scaffolding to help students develop the independent learning skills needed to succeed can lead to extremely powerful educational experiences where students are intrinsically motivated to engage their highest cognitive abilities.

Encouraging Students' Cognitive and Affective Progress

Educators (both teaching faculty and librarians) can promote students' cognitive and affective progress in several ways. The first thing that educators can do is to scaffold the necessary procedural skills before students begin independent work on a writing-from-sources assignment. For lower-level classes, this most likely means modeling skills such as how to read the type of texts the assignment requires and giving students several opportunities for meaningful practice with feedback on their performance. For upper-level students, this may be advanced practice in synthesizing information from multiple sources, again through modeling and practice activities.

Good assignment design in writing-from-sources assignments is critical for students to produce the quality of critical thinking, inquiry, reading, and writing required for true transformation of knowledge. Such an assignment would include a focus on students' *process*. The resulting mini assignments should be designed as authentically as possible so that they create a more seamless learning experience for students.

The final method educators can employ to encourage students' progress is through formative assessment, or "in-the-process-of-learning assessments."[50] Formative assessment is closely tied with increasing motivation, self-efficacy, and direction.[51] One of the most important aspects of formative assessment is its focus on timely individual feedback. Because the kind of writing-from-sources assignments this book promotes are process-focused, there are numerous opportunities for formative assessment and meaningful feedback. During the process, students' low-stakes writing provides concrete evidence of their current status and understanding, to which educators and their peers can respond to promote progress in the cognitive domains of learning as well as motivation and encouragement in the affective domains.

A Theory of Process-Based Information Literacy

The product-focused nature of the traditional research paper is so deeply taken for granted in higher education that educators can no longer see such assignments objectively. A combination of composition specialists and librarians had already begun to criticize how the ACRL's *Standards* have an implicitly strong focus on the research product even before drafts of the *Framework* began to emerge.[52] Since the release of the *Framework*'s drafts, others have started to echo this sentiment, including Critten and Seeber in their ACRL 2015 conference presentation.[53] These scholars pointed out that the five standards imply individual stages of the research process that must each be completed before the next begins (figure 2.1).

FIGURE 2.1
ACRL's *Information Literacy Competency Standards* as a linear process

The individual standards do not make sense in any order other than that in which they are presented. ACRL even has a supporting webpage entitled "The Standards: Step-by-Step" that states the *Standards* have a "logical hierarchy."[54] The focus of information literacy framed by the *Standards* is on information sources, papers, and grades. This does not reflect the way professional research and writing actually happens. Instruction librarians teach information literacy in a way that neither librarians nor the professors they work with actually practice. It is imaginary and impossible, detached from both reality and the critical-thinking, creativity, reading, and writing skills that students must perform in order to successfully complete the assignment.

The LIS literature demonstrates a need to make information literacy instruction more meaningful. Leckie asserts that the process in which many research paper assignments are conducted "is flawed from beginning to end," and she questions whether such assignments further students' understanding in the field.[55] More recent studies, such as Holliday and colleagues, show that students are not meeting educators' expectations, but the researchers do not indicate *where* students' processes are going awry.[56] Bivens-Tatum, Fister, and Bean and Iyer criticize librarians for placing too much focus on *finding* information.[57] Bivens-Tatum writes, "The actual library searching portion of most student research essays is a small part of what they're learning to do, and not the most important part."[58] Fister is concerned that librarians' overemphasis on retrieval systems implies to students the assignment is collecting parts of information, not "construct[ing] a text."[59] She can find no positive evidence in the literature, and indeed she cites one study that showed a negative relation, that finding good sources is more likely to create better papers. Bivens-Tatum and Fister emphasize that teaching information literacy would be more effective if it were more embedded in what is known about inquiry and rhetoric.

Academic librarians frequently attempt to align themselves with the social sciences, at least for research methodologies.[60] However, librarians have much to learn about their own field from scholars in the disciplines of composition, reading, and rhetoric. Scholars in these fields have been analyzing how people make meaning through reading and writing and how scholars make and communicate knowledge over vast amounts of time and distance. For example, they frequently stress that a thesis question generally solidifies fairly late in the inquiry process, although librarians tend to like well-defined research questions up front. One fundamental aspect of information literacy that librarians can learn from scholars in these fields is how to support students in extending this period of ambiguity as this is where much of the learning from such assignments occurs.

Mazziotti and Grettano found that the ACRL's *Information Literacy Competency Standards for Higher Education* aligned quite closely with the *WPA* (Writing Program Administrators) *Outcomes for First Year Composition*, although the *Standards* were clearly more product-focused.[61] Norgaard, a rhetorician, argues that information literacy suffers from two misperceptions: that it is only "functional or performative" and that it is a "neutral, discrete, context-free skill."[62] He points out that rhetoric and composition departments have traditionally faced the same misperceptions. He goes on to argue that "information literacy informed by work in rhetoric and composition would help yield a more situated, process-oriented literacy relevant to a broad range of rhetorical and intellectual activities."[63]

Composition specialists have long known that focusing on the process of writing is the only way to significantly improve both the quality of learning and the quality of writing in students' research papers. Very few authors in the LIS literature have touched on the messy and iterative nature of research. Nutefall and Ryder write, "It is important for librarians and faculty to recognize that students need to experience the uncertainty and anxiety inherent in research."[64] Morgan points out that librarians must recognize and teach that "there's a lot of fail in research,"[65] which even the LIS articles on inquiry do not appropriately acknowledge. Librarians must begin on a profession-wide scale to work with teaching faculty to discover how they can better support students through the chaos that is research.

In order to support process-focused writing-from-sources assignments, librarians must develop a processed-focused theory of information literacy. During the *Framework* revision process, the six individual frames were reordered between publicly released drafts, a clear demonstration that they have no sequential order. Two of the frames, "Research as Inquiry" and "Searching as Strategic Exploration," particularly emphasize the iterative nature of research. The *Framework* has inspired new discussions about what a process-based concept of information literacy would look like. However, to date such a concept is underdeveloped, and the adoption of the *Framework* can do only so much by itself to fundamentally change the profession's approach to teaching information literacy. A process-based information literacy model must have several critical attributes, which will be discussed in the remainder of this chapter.

1. Keep Information Literacy within the Context of the Overall Assignment

Information literacy should not be taught in a silo. Brady and colleagues and Artman and colleagues criticize how research is taught as an isolated skill, which is undoubtedly due to the limitations of the one-shot information literacy instruction model, at least in part.[66] Morgan criticizes the poor assignments he sees from teaching faculty, such as requirements to write some kind of research paper based on a certain number of a particular kind of source.[67] He says that he feels "torn between the expectations of the instructor, the practical tools students need to be able to use and anything remotely conceptual I'd like to get them thinking about."[68] Critten and Seeber say that librarians are setting students up for failure when they agree to teach "a bad thing badly."[69]

With the exception of those librarians who teach for-credit information literacy courses, a situation that has its own issues, process-based information literacy instruction must begin with process-based assignments designed by teaching faculty. These are the assignments that, among other things, embrace many types of low-stakes writing that will be discussed in chapter 3. Librarians can play a role in influencing assignment design, which they already have a history of doing. This requires deep levels of collaboration between librarians and teaching faculty, which can be developed only over time.

2. Emphasize the Inseparable Relationship between Reading and Writing

Process-based information literacy instruction must provide a more accurate picture of the inseparable nature of reading and writing in the writing-from-sources process. The common perception of the research process is that a student picks a topic, develops a thesis, reads, writes, then edits surface features before turning in the paper. However, this is not how real research happens, and therefore it should not be what students are taught.

Just as professional researchers use writing to figure out what they want to say as they join a scholarly conversation, students need to use low-stakes writing to discover and refine their topic and find personal interest in it. Chapter 4 will provide information on useful low-stakes writing activities that students can use to improve and support reading comprehension as they read their information sources. They can also be encouraged to engage in reflective writing, outlines, and drafts *while they continue to read their information sources*, which will be explored in chapters 3 and 5. Such writing will trigger critical thinking and direct their information-seeking and reading activities. Trying to separate reading and writing is artificial, inefficient, and ultimately ineffective. Good writing-from-sources assignment design will encourage written evidence of reading comprehension and synthesis of information from multiple sources. Such assignments will break up a difficult task in meaningful and authentic ways in order to spread out the cognitive load. More information will be provided about using low-stakes writing throughout the writing-from-sources process in chapters 3, 4, and 5.

3. Encourage Both the Cognitive and Affective Aspects of Inquiry

Educators are primarily concerned with what a student knows or can do as a result of instruction, which represents the cognitive aspect of learning. Yet if educators ignore the affective aspects of learning and writing-from-sources, students will not achieve the cognitive benefits of such assignments. This means that educators need to understand what the cognitive and affective aspects of inquiry are and how to support them. This is not an easy task, and there is very little in the LIS literature to support such learning because it has not been a common aspect of librarians' approach to information literacy instruction.

Nearly two decades apart, Fister and Bivens-Tatum both point out that librarians want students to come to the classroom and the reference desk with well-formed questions, but that is not a realistic expectation of what students should know at the beginning of the inquiry process.[70] They argue that librarians should do a better job in supporting true inquiry, including the prolonged ambiguity. Morgan points out that information literacy should be useful beyond the confines of students' undergraduate careers and that in teaching information literacy, "We should actually be enabling a kind of do-it-yourself (DIY) epistemological inquiry."[71] Librarians need to learn to support students in the early stages of chaos when they do not have a defined information need and are therefore feeling insecure and anxious.

In 1986, Mellon coined the term *library anxiety*.[72] She observed that "many students became so anxious that they are unable to approach the problem logically or effectively."[73] Kulthau's model of the information search process also focuses on the affective side of research.[74] While her stages involve what students *know* about their topic and their goal at a given point in the process, there is a strong emphasis on the *feelings* they are likely to experience at each stage. Schroeder and Cahoy begin to explore how information literacy standards can incorporate affect in library learning.[75] These are the most seminal works in the LIS literature that validate the affective aspects of information literacy and discuss how such feelings encourage or discourage cognitive progress in the research process.

While there is information in the LIS literature about the affective aspects of research, more is needed to demonstrate how they influence the cognitive aspects. For example, how can librarians work with teaching faculty to promote intrinsic motivation in the form of curiosity? How can librarians model and convey the messy process of inquiry in various information literacy instruction contexts? How can librarians who provide reference services assist students who are still in the ambiguous stages of research where they do not have well-defined research questions? These are just some of the questions that academic librarians should begin asking themselves, each other, and teaching faculty in order to support students' motivation and cognitive development through writing-from-sources assignments.

4. Include Meaningful Process-Based Assessments That the Librarian Has Access To

Process-based writing-from-sources assignments will naturally involve process-based learning activities that can double as formative assessments. This may come in the form of research logs, reflective writing, mind maps, notes, annotated bibliographies, outlines, and drafts. Mimicking the types of low-stakes and mid-stakes writing activities that experienced writers create for themselves will allow educators to have a window into the thought processes of students, discourage procrastination and plagiarism, and provide an opportunity for timely feedback to further students' learning.

One of the key qualities of formative assessments is that they must be done in a safe learning environment where learners are encouraged to test out new understandings without fear of mistakes being reflected in their grades. Process-based assessments should be *assessed*, but not *graded* for anything other than effort and participation. Hafer writes, "Student writers need our language to supply them the energy that works toward superior writing. We cannot supply that strengthening language if we are spending— no, wasting—all our feedback energies on grading their writing."[76] Grades bring closure; feedback encourages improvement and continued learning. While Hafer admits that grades must eventually be given, he argues the time and energy an educator spends on supporting the writing (and inquiry) process is better spent on "low stakes responding and conferencing."[77]

It is critical for librarians to be included on at least some of these assessments for the assignments they support. Librarians must have access to evidence of what students are doing in relation to the instruction the librarians provide and an opportunity to provide their own constructive feedback. Having a librarian give feedback provides students with another perspective on information use and may be pitched to teaching faculty as a way to share the workload of such feedback. What this means for the workload of the librarian will be briefly addressed in chapter 6. Whether or not librarians have collaborative relationships with teaching faculty, they can still conduct process-based assessments, although they may be limited to the ones that fit within the library one-shot instruction session.

5. Provide Support for Making Meaning from the Information the Library Provides

As this book will explore in chapter 4, the modern American education system provides very little support for developing reading comprehension skills after elementary school. Furthermore, the texts that educators ask students to locate and read for college-level research papers are usually quite difficult even for professional researchers with a great deal of background knowledge and intrinsic motivation. The literature on reading comprehension skills in college students is sympathetic to students who struggle in this area.[78]

Librarians can become more aware of basic reading comprehension theory, particularly how students draw on their existing schemata to construct meaning through reading informational texts with an eye on their own rhetorical goals. Such knowledge will enable librarians to better assist students in making meaning from their sources, which is inseparable from evaluating those sources. As Kulthau points out, librarians must stop viewing and teaching "relevance as a static entity [which] severely limits understanding the dynamic process of formulating a problem or learning about a subject."[79] Instead, users incorporate new information into what they already know, which is a dynamic and personal process of knowledge construction. Kulthau goes on to argue, "Library services based exclusively on a source-location premise are constrained in situations that call for mediation in the constructive process of users."[80] The reading comprehension theory described later in this book will help librarians better understand and support the dynamic process of meaning making that happens in well-designed writing-from-sources assignments.

6. Remember that Information Literacy Learning Must Happen over Time

Stilling writes, "It is possible that students' less-than-satisfactory work stemmed from the fact that the research—as well as the writing—was done only a day or two before the assignment was due. I believe that one of the primary factors in poor performance on research-based assignments is procrastination."[81] Like many compositionists such as Hafer, Stilling also points out that another benefit of dragging the writing-from-sources process out over time is that it distributes the considerable cognitive load of such assignments.[82] It also allows the brain to "percolate." According to Carey, the human brain continues to work on problems, such as those in a writing-from-sources assignment, even when one is doing other things.[83] If educators force students to spread the process over time, students will have more time to percolate and develop more complex thinking.

Likewise, the librarian's responsibility in teaching process-based information literacy cannot be adequately done in the information literacy one-shot session. I have had a number of discussions with instruction librarians during the development of this book. I have asked them questions such as "How do you teach the messy inquiry process?" and "How does your own writing influence how you teach information literacy?" In all cases, these librarians have expressed how much more they would like to do, but that they cannot teach such things in the confines of the one-shot session. In some cases, they scale what they would like to teach down, simply scratching the surface of something meaningful. In other cases, they limit their wealth of knowledge based on reflecting on their own professional writing to providing authentic anecdotes and empathy to students. Process-based information literacy instruction must be spread out within courses and departmental curriculums.

Reflections on Process-Based Information Literacy

Looking at this list, it is clear that moving to a process-based theory of information literacy will require librarians to step out of traditional librarian roles focusing on searching for information and evaluating sources superficially. This may involve taking on new roles such as teaching reading comprehension, concept mapping, synthesis, rhetorical evaluation, context, problem solving, and metacognition. This is a particular challenge as librarians are few in number compared to the number of teaching faculty and students at their institutions. Breaking into new roles will require careful strategic thinking and will likely look very different from one campus to the next.

The conversation of process-based information literacy was begun by others several decades ago but has not been well developed. Librarians and teaching faculty will agree that too few undergraduate students achieve the educational goals of the research paper. The educational theories presented in this chapter and elaborated on throughout this book begin to shed light on solutions to the problem. These are theories that have been in existence for a long time but have not been widespread outside of their own disciplines and certainly not within librarianship. It is important for librarians to thoroughly immerse themselves in such theory and the related empirical research before looking for practical ways to make it their own.

Notes

1.   Ian Beilin, "Beyond the Threshold: Conformity, Resistance, and the ACRL Information Literacy Framework for Higher Education," *In the Library with the Lead*

Pipe, February 25, 2015, http://www.inthelibrarywiththeleadpipe.org/2015/beyond-the-threshold-conformity-resistance-and-the-aclr-information-literacy-framework-for-higher-education.

2. Elaine P. Maimon, Barbara F. Nodine, and Finbarr W. O'Connor, *Thinking, Reasoning, and Writing* (New York: Longman, 1989); Richard Menary, "Writing as Thinking," *Language Sciences* 29, no. 5 (2007): 621–32; Donald Morison Murray, *A Writer Teaches Writing: A Practical Method of Teaching Composition*, 2nd ed. (Boston: Houghton Mifflin, 1985).

3. John Dewey, *Democracy and Education: An Introduction to the Philosophy of Education* (New York: Macmillan, 1916).

4. David Elkind, "Piaget, Jean (1896–1980)," in *The Encyclopedia of Education*, ed. James W. Guthrie, 2nd ed., vol. 5 (New York: Macmillan Reference USA, 2003), 1894–98.

5. Margaret E. Gredler, "Vygotsky, Lev (1896–1934)," in *The Encyclopedia of Education*, ed. James W. Guthrie, 2nd ed., vol. 7 (New York: Macmillan Reference USA, 2003), 2658–60.

6. Richard C. Anderson, "The Notion of Schemata and the Educational Enterprise: General Discussion of the Conference," in *Schooling and the Acquisition of Knowledge*, ed. Richard C. Anderson, Rand J. Spiro, and William E. Montague (Hillsdale, NJ: Lawrence Erlbaum Associates, 1977), 415–31; Doug Brent, *Reading as Rhetorical Invention: Knowledge, Persuasion, and the Teaching of Research-Based Writing* (Urbana, IL: National Council of Teachers of English, 1992).

7. Mortimer Jerome Adler and Charles Van Doren, *How to Read a Book*, rev. and updated ed. (New York: Simon and Schuster, 1972).

8. Donald Morison Murray, *Learning by Teaching: Selected Articles on Writing and Teaching* (Montclair, NJ: Boynton/Cook, 1982); Linda Flower, *Problem-Solving Strategies for Writing*, 4th ed. (New York: Harcourt Brace Jovanovich, 1993).

9. John C. Bean and Nalini Iyer, "'I Couldn't Find an Article That Answered My Question': Teaching the Construction of Meaning in Undergraduate Literary Research," in *Teaching Literary Research: Challenges in a Changing Environment*, ed. Kathleen A. Johnson and Steven R. Harris (Chicago: Association of College and Research Libraries, 2009), 22–40.

10. John Sweller, Paul L. Ayres, and Slava Kalyuga, *Cognitive Load Theory* (New York: Springer, 2011).

11. Barbara A. Dosher, "Working Memory," in *Encyclopedia of Cognitive Science*, vol. 4, ed. Lynn Nadel (Hoboken, NJ: Wiley, 2005), 569.

12. Ronald Thomas Kellogg, *The Psychology of Writing* (New York: Oxford University Press, 1994).

13. S. T. Perrault, "Cognition and Error in Student Writing," *Journal on Excellence in College Teaching* 22, no. 3 (2011): 47–73; Gary R. Hafer, *Embracing Writing: Ways to Teach Reluctant Writers in Any College Course* (San Francisco: Jossey-Bass, 2014).

14. Ronald T. Kellogg and Bascom A. Raulerson, "Improving the Writing Skills of College Students," *Psychonomic Bulletin and Review* 14, no. 2 (2007): 237.

15. Sweller, Ayres, and Kalyuga, *Cognitive Load Theory*.

16. Ibid., 58.

17. Ibid.

18. Ibid.

19. Ruth Schoenbach, Cynthia Greenleaf, Christine Cziko, and Lori Hurwitz, *Reading for*

Understanding: A Guide to Improving Reading in Middle and High School Classrooms (San Francisco: Jossey-Bass, 1999).

20. Peter Elbow, *Vernacular Eloquence: What Speech Can Bring to Writing* (Oxford: Oxford University Press, 2012); Flower, *Problem-Solving Strategies for Writing.*

21. Dewey, *Democracy and Education.*

22. Maria de la Luz Perez and Russell Binkley, "Self-Efficacy," in *The Greenwood Dictionary of Education*, ed. John William Collins and Nancy P. O'Brien (Westport, CT: Greenwood Press, 2003), 319.

23. Albert Bandura, "Adolescent Development from an Agentic Perspective," in *Self-Efficacy Beliefs of Adolescents*, ed. Frank Pajares and Timothy C. Urdan (Greenwich, CT: Information Age, 2006), 1–43.

24. Ibid.

25. Ibid.

26. Albert Bandura, Claudio Barbaranelli, Gian Vittorio Caprara, and Concetta Pastorelli, "Multifaceted Impact of Self-Efficacy Beliefs on Academic Functioning," *Child Development* 67, no. 3 (1996), 1206.

27. Frank Pajares, "Overview of Social Cognitive Theory and of Self-Efficacy," 2002, accessed August 15, 2016, http://www.uky.edu/~eushe2/Pajares/eff.html.

28. Frank Pajares, "Current Directions in Self-Efficacy Research," in *Advances in Motivation and Achievement*, ed. Martin L. Maehr and Paul R. Pintrich, vol. 10 (Greenwich, CT: JAI Press, 1997), 1–49.

29. Albert Bandura, "Self-Efficacy," in *Encyclopedia of Human Behavior*, ed. V. S. Ramachaudran, vol. 4 (New York: Academic Press. 1994), 71–81; Pajares, "Overview of Social Cognitive Theory."

30. Pajares, "Overview of Social Cognitive Theory," 6.

31. Bandura, "Self-Efficacy"; Pajares, "Overview of Social Cognitive Theory."

32. Bandura, "Self-Efficacy"; Pajares, "Overview of Social Cognitive Theory."

33. Bandura, "Self-Efficacy."

34. Pajares, "Overview of Social Cognitive Theory."

35. Ibid.

36. Bandura, "Self-Efficacy"; Pajares, "Overview of Social Cognitive Theory."

37. Pajares, "Overview of Social Cognitive Theory."

38. Dewey, *Democracy and Education.*

39. Evelyn R. Oka, "Motivation," in *Encyclopedia of School Psychology*, ed. Steven W. Lee (Thousand Oaks, CA: Sage Publications, 2005), 330.

40. Ibid., 332.

41. Toby Fulwiler, *College Writing: A Personal Approach to Academic Writing* (Portsmouth, NH: Boynton/Cook, 1997), 53.

42. Ian Leslie, *Curious: The Desire to Know and Why Your Future Depends on It* (New York: Basic Books, 2014), xx.

43. Ibid.

44. Ibid., 87.

45. Susan M. Leist, *Writing to Teach; Writing to Learn in Higher Education* (Lanham, MD: University Press of America, 2006), 83.

46. John C. Bean, *Engaging Ideas: The Professor's Guide to Integrating Writing, Critical Thinking, and Active Learning in the Classroom* (San Francisco: Jossey-Bass, 1996).

47. Leslie, *Curious.*

48. Bean, *Engaging Ideas*, 31.

49. Oka, "Motivation."

50. Eva L. Baker and Girly C. Delacruz, "Framework for the Assessment of Learning in Games," in *Computer Games and Team and Individual Learning*, ed. Harold F. O'Neil and Ray S. Perez (London: Elsevier, 2007), 21–37.

51. Susan Brookhart, Connie Moss, and Beverly Long, "Formative Assessment That Empowers," *Educational Leadership* 66, no. 3 (2008): 52–57.

52. Rolf Norgaard, "Writing Information Literacy: Contributions to a Concept," *Reference and User Services Quarterly* 43, no. 2 (2003): 124–30; Patrick K. Morgan, "Information Literacy Learning as Epistemological Process," *Reference Services Review* 42, no. 3 (2014): 403–13; Donna Mazziotti and Teresa Grettano, "'Hanging Together': Collaboration between Information Literacy and Writing Programs Based on the ACRL Standards and the WPA Outcomes" (presentation, ACRL 2011 Conference, Philadelphia, PA, March 30–April 2, 2011), http://www.ala.org/acrl/sites/ala.org.acrl/files/content/conferences/confsandpreconfs/national/2011/papers/hanging_together.pdf.

53. Jessica Critten and Kevin Seeber, "Process, Not Product: Teaching and Assessing the Critical Process of Information Literacy" (presentation, Association of College and Research Libraries Conference, Portland, OR, March 27, 2015).

54. Association of College and Research Libraries, "The Standards: Step-by-Step," accessed August 15, 2016, http://www.ala.org/acrl/issues/infolit/standards/steps.

55. Gloria J. Leckie, "Desperately Seeking Citations: Uncovering Faculty Assumptions about the Undergraduate Research Process," *Journal of Academic Librarianship* 22, no. 3 (1996): 201.

56. Wendy Holliday, Betty Dance, Erin Davis, Britt Fagerheim, Anne Hedrich, Kacy Lundstrom, and Pamela Martin, "An Information Literacy Snapshot: Authentic Assessment across the Curriculum," *College and Research Libraries* 76, no. 2 (2015): 170–87.

57. Wayne Bivens-Tatum, "Timing of the Research Question," *Academic Librarian: On Libraries, Rhetoric, Poetry, History, and Moral Philosophy* (blog), November 30, 2010, https://blogs.princeton.edu/librarian/2010/11/timing_of_the_research_question; Barbara Fister, "Teaching the Rhetorical Dimensions of Research," *Research Strategies* 11, no. 4 (1993): 211–19; Bean and Iyer, "'I Couldn't Find an Article That Answered My Question.'"

58. Bivens-Tatum, "Timing of the Research Question."

59. Fister, "Teaching the Rhetorical Dimensions of Research," 212.

60. Heidi L. M. Jacobs and Denise Koufogiannakis, "Counting What Cannot Be Counted: Bringing the Humanities to EBLIP," *Evidence Based Library and Information Practice* 9, no. 3 (2014): 110–20.

61. Mazziotti and Grettano, "'Hanging Together.'"

62. Norgaard, "Writing Information Literacy," 125.

63. Ibid.

64. Jennifer E. Nutefall and Phyllis Mentzell Ryder, "The Timing of the Research Question: First-Year Writing Faculty and Instruction Librarians' Differing Perspectives," *portal: Libraries and the Academy* 10, no. 4 (2010): 444.

65. Morgan, "Information Literacy Learning as Epistemological Process," 405.

66. Laura Brady, Nathalie Singh-Corcoran, Jo Ann Dadisman, and Kelly Diamond, "A Collaborative Approach to Information Literacy: First-Year Composition, Writing Center, and Library Partnerships at West Virginia University," *Composition Forum* 19

(Spring 2009), http://compositionforum.com/issue/19/west-virginia.php; Margaret Artman, Erica Frisicaro-Pawlowski, and Robert Monge, "Not Just One Shot: Extending the Dialogues about Information Literacy in Composition Classes," *Composition Studies* 38, no. 2 (2010): 93–110.

67. Morgan, "Information Literacy Learning as Epistemological Process."
68. Ibid., 407.
69. Critten and Seeber, "Process, Not Product."
70. Fister, "Teaching the Rhetorical Dimensions of Research"; Bivens-Tatum, "Timing of the Research Question."
71. Morgan, "Information Literacy Learning as Epistemological Process," 405.
72. Constance A. Mellon, "Library Anxiety: A Grounded Theory and Its Development," *College and Research Libraries* 47, no. 2 (1986): 160–65.
73. Ibid., 163.
74. Carol Collier Kulthau, *Seeking Meaning: A Process Approach to Library and Information Services*, 2nd ed. (Westport, CT: Libraries Unlimited, 2004).
75. Robert Schroeder and Ellysa Stern Cahoy, "Valuing Information Literacy: Affective Learning and the ACRL Standards," *portal: Libraries and the Academy* 10, no. 2 (2010): 127–46.
76. Hafer, *Embracing Writing*, 207.
77. Ibid., 208.
78. Adler and Van Doren, *How to Read a Book*; Bean, *Engaging Ideas*; Rebecca Moore Howard, Tricia Serviss, and Tanya K. Rodrigue, "Writing from Sources, Writing from Sentences," *Writing and Pedagogy* 2, no. 2 (2010): 177–92.
79. Kulthau, *Seeking Meaning*, 3.
80. Ibid., 5.
81. Glenn Ellen Starr Stilling, "Beyond the Research Paper: Working with Faculty to Maximize Library-Related Assignments," in *Integrating Information Literacy into the College Experience: Papers Presented at the Thirtieth LOEX Library Instruction Conference*, ed. Julia K. Nims, Randal Baier, Rita Bullard, and Eric Owen (Ann Arbor, MI: Pierian Press, 2003), 34.
82. Hafer, *Embracing Writing*. Stilling, "Beyond the Research Paper."
83. Benedict Carey, *How We Learn: The Surprising Truth about When, Where, and Why It Happens* (New York: Random House, 2014).

CHAPTER 3

Informal, Low-Stakes Writing

In French, the word for a rough draft is brouillon, derived from a verb meaning "to place in disorder, to scramble...." This metaphor suggests a writing process that begins as a journey into disorder, a making of chaos, out of which one eventually forges an essay.

—Bean[1]

Librarians can take advantage of low-stakes, informal writing activities to encourage process-based information literacy. Low-stakes writing is not part of only the *writing* process, but also the *thinking* process. Despite the common advice to "think before you write," expert writers use writing to generate and enhance thinking. In fact, many writing scholars say that *writing is thinking.*[2] Behind polished pieces of thoughtful and clear prose is a great deal of hard, messy, and frequently frustrating mental work. Writing is a catalyst for creativity, problem solving, critical thinking, and making meaning. This is a lot to demand of the human brain and too much to demand of the brain to do all at once. Good formal writing is almost always a result of a lot of informal writing that is rarely seen by anyone other than the author.

Low-stakes writing can slow the research process down in order to allow more time for reflection and critical thinking, something that several LIS authors encourage. Koppelman says that slowing down the research process will "return... the pleasure, seduction, and delight which is due to it."[3] Lundstrom and colleagues and Holliday and colleagues changed their instruction to encourage students to slow down and reflect more during the research process.[4] This chapter will look at how low-stakes writing can slow down the research process to encourage knowledge transformation and solid writing-from-sources papers.

Process, Creativity, and Low-Stakes Writing

The problems with undergraduate writing are well known among educators, as was explored in chapter 1. In his book *Embracing Writing*, Hafer introduces what he calls the "Writing Problem," which focuses less on what is wrong with student writing than what is wrong with the educational system that fosters such disappointing writing by students.[5] He goes on to explain that the Writing Problem has four parts:

1. School teaches that good writing is writing without errors.
2. School writing is high-stakes writing.
3. Low-stakes writing is seen as a waste of time.
4. Writing is treated as a second subject teachers do not have the time or expertise to teach in content classrooms.

Hafer spends a good part of his book arguing that good high-stakes writing can be achieved in no other way than through low-stakes writing. He says, "When we characterize any academic writing as bad, we can just as accurately call it premature or unfinished."[6] All writers, no matter what their level of experience, need a safe place to lay out their ideas and, over time, shape those ideas into something worth sharing with others. According to Hafer, low-stakes writing helps writers of all kinds use writing to overcome the Writing Problem. While Hafer is not specifically talking about the writing-from-sources that librarians are concerned with, one can easily apply each of these four aspects of the Writing Problem to writing-from-sources.

As was described in chapter 1, writing-from-sources is hard work for many reasons. One must negotiate between personal symbols (thoughts) and consensual symbols (words) when reading and writing and figure out how pieces of information relate to one another or with one's previous knowledge.[7] Furthermore, the kinds of research questions teaching faculty want students to pose in writing-from-sources assignments are usually ill-structured, without easy answers. Through writing-from-sources, writers construct new understandings on the subject about which they are writing, but this is a gradual and messy process.

It is perhaps easier to understand why writing is so hard when one realizes that *to write* is *to create*, and that *creating* is the highest point in the Revised Bloom's Taxonomy.[8] Good writing-from-sources assignments require students to create something *new* as opposed to simply reporting what others have written on the subject. Many educators may question whether knowledge *creation* is possible among undergraduate students, but educators can draw on the literature on creativity to rethink what is meant by "new." Boden points out that the novelty of an idea to an individual is still valuable even if the idea has occurred to countless other people in the past.[9] In assembling their own unique combinations of ideas from the ideas of others, students are creating something that is new to them. In other words, they are learning through creativity, which seems much more achievable for undergraduate students than asking them to create something completely novel to the discipline.

As previously mentioned in this chapter, the literature on low-stakes writing and creativity emphasizes a need for writers to have a safe psychological space to experiment without fear of consequences or criticism.[10] Such safe spaces encourage learners (both novice and expert) to take risks, practice divergent thinking, experiment, and learn through failure. For scientists, such a place is oftentimes in a laboratory, where one does not expect the first experiment to be a success. For actors, musicians, and athletes, this is time spent in rehearsal or practice. For a writer, such a place is *always* found in low-stakes writing because it is (usually) private.[11] For experienced writers, the primary audience of low-stakes writing is themselves. It is a place where they can explore initial thoughts, develop ideas, make connections, gradually construct meaning and knowledge, and sometimes come to terms with the affective aspects of the writing process without fear of others' judgment. Elbow encourages writers to think about freewriting as "speaking to the page," which allows writers to get their ideas more fluidly onto paper or screen.[12] He says that the benefits of private writing include producing a greater quantity of writing to revise, being able to devote one's full attention to developing ideas for the purpose of communication, safety, ownership, and developing one's voice. He argues that most writing is in fact private, even among expert writers. Only a very small amount of what is written is ever shared with others.

Several authors have discussed how focusing on the writing process, including the vast amounts of informal writing that go into a finished piece, have helped them to develop confidence and to love writing. Elbow writes, "When I realized that my early drafts were in fact private, my process of producing them changed, becoming much more adventuresome and productive—much less anxious."[13] Flower describes her own affective transformation as a writer:

I didn't begin to actively enjoy writing—to feel secretly excited about the time I spend thinking at the typewriter—until I stopped seeing my writing as a polished, finished product. With that "finished product" perspective, the only way to succeed was to sound as elegant and authoritative as the published writers I was reading. And somehow I never did. The pleasure came when I began concentrating on what I wanted to accomplish and trying to figure out how to do it.[14]

If expert writers spread out the cognitive load of writing and also find confidence and enjoyment in the writing-from-sources process, educators can also emphasize this process in writing-from-sources assignments to develop these attitudes among students. This includes incorporating low-stakes writing into one's assignment design, devoting class time to low-stakes writing, and providing formative feedback on low-stakes writing assignments (assessing students' low-stakes writing will be explored later in this chapter).

Types of Low-Stakes Writing

It helps one to understand what low-stakes writing is by looking at some common examples. Low-stakes writing comes in many forms, and each has different qualities and potential uses depending on one's purpose for writing. All of these examples are useful for writing-from-sources. Examples of the various formats of low-stakes writing include

- **Drafting:** The messy process of generating and refining ideas and words into more formal pieces of writing. The drafts themselves are considered low-stakes or mid-stakes writing and should be embraced as such. Early drafts are frequently confused and disorganized. As drafting involves transformation through revision and rewriting, it is distinct among the other types of low-stakes writing discussed in this chapter and will be addressed in more detail in chapter 5.
- **Freewriting:** Writing about whatever comes to mind. There is no editing and no criticism. One is even free to write about how empty one's mind is at the moment. The purpose of this technique is simply to produce nonstop, prolific writing. Hafer recommends timed freewriting, especially when one is stuck.[15] In this technique, writers set a fixed amount of time, such as ten

minutes, and do not allow themselves to quit writing until that ten minutes is complete.

- **Journaling or daily writing:** A systematic way of keeping track of one's thoughts. Fulwiler cites a number of studies that argue "human beings find meaning in the world by exploring it through language—through their own easy talky language, not the language of textbook and teacher."[16] Journal entries are usually dated and kept in a notebook. Fulwiler says that journals can be a place where a learner can observe, define, wonder, speculate, and connect ideas and meanings.[17] According to Hafer, daily writing tends to be less personal than journaling.[18] Daily writing may also motivate some reluctant writers to actually write *daily*. Regardless of the difference between journaling and daily writing, both of these practices get writers to write frequently and create a record of the work that is taking place in their minds.

- **Mind mapping, concept mapping, or sketchnoting:** "Rich visual notes created from a mix of handwriting, drawings, hand-drawn typography, shapes, and visual elements like arrows, boxes and lines."[19] They are "built from meaningful thoughts and ideas your mind collects and squirrels away"[20] and can be used to create real-time or retrospective notes of lectures, make meaning from readings, brainstorm, make an inventory of ideas and knowledge, and identify relationships between ideas. Additionally, mind mapping is useful because unlike writing (high- or low-stakes), which must be linear, mind maps allow writers to branch meaning in all directions. This allows them to push linear organization to a later point in the writing process.

- **Note-taking:** External storage for information learned. As the human brain can store and retrieve only so much information at a time, the easiest way to relieve one's cognitive load limitations while retaining important information is to store new information externally, whether it is in a notebook, on Post-It notes, on index cards, or in a digital file.[21] Notes primarily focus on information external to the writer, such as lectures or readings of texts. However, notes are also good places to capture one's immediate responses to such information, such as making connections to other texts, experiences, or one's current rhetorical goal.

- **Annotated bibliographies:** Notes from information sources such as texts or lectures reworked to be shared with others. This is a common mini assignment in preparation for a formal research paper. According to Bean, an annotated bibliography assignment is most productive if students are required to include a summary, an evaluation of the source's quality, and a description of how it is useful to their rhetorical goal.[22] This encourages students to read their sources rhetorically, thinking about what the text's author is trying to say while also making a plan to utilize the information when it is their turn to write.

- **Outlining:** The skeletons of prose. Outlines are useful to organize ideas into sequential order, but they should evolve throughout the drafting process as writers figure out what they want to say. Outlines are useful throughout the writing process, not only in the initial stages of drafting. Reverse outlines, where one creates an outline from written prose, can reveal problems in structure, organization, flow, or coverage of the topic, which may not otherwise be apparent.

- **Reflective writing or postwriting:** A useful tool for students to reflect on something they just experienced or learned. Reflection helps a learner transform experience into knowledge.[23] Thus, it also helps get students ready for their next learning experience. Furthermore, such writing is a powerful educational tool that allows educators to see what students are thinking or how they experienced a learning activity. Postwriting in the form of an exam or project "wrapper" can provide a student with a place to reflect on how he or she could have performed better, again preparing the student for improved performance in the future.[24] Such evidence of student thought processes may also help educators improve teaching and assignments over time.

This list of low-stakes writing formats is in no way comprehensive. Low-stakes writing can include many other formats such as lists, index cards, and sketches. The important characteristics all of these formats share is that they are colloquial, speech-like (if even words at all), often riddled with grammatical errors and questions, and frequently use first-person pronouns to aid the writer in making meaning from a combination of internal and external information.[25]

Purposes of Low-Stakes Writing

In educational contexts, informal writing is a powerful tool in teaching source-based writing, as it promotes critical thinking and reflection and opens avenues for educators to provide individual, point-of-need assistance to each learner. Low-stakes writing serves four primary purposes in writing-from-sources and its instruction: spreading out the considerable cognitive load of formal writing; making thought visible for oneself; making thought visible for evaluation by educators; and finally, informal writing may be the key to students achieving intrinsic motivation to write from sources. Acknowledging these four reasons not only provides an argument for why educators should assign low-stakes writing, but also suggests how to maximize the educational potential of such assignments.

1. Distributing Cognitive Load

Writing-from-sources is an activity that requires a great deal of cognitive resources. As was seen from cognitive load theory in chapter 2, such resources are limited. Kellogg writes, "Writing is a particularly demanding activity, because various cognitive, metacognitive, and linguistic processes must be coordinated. A student who is assigned a writing task has to make decisions not only about what and how to write, but also about the use of time, the selection of sources to gain information, the strategies to be adopted, and so on."[26]

While Hollywood films have fueled a romanticized view of a gifted writer cranking out a novel, expert writers spread out the cognitive load of writing over time through the various forms of low-stakes writing explored in the previous section of this chapter.

Hafer, a rhetoric professor at Lycoming College, frequently starts faculty workshops with an exercise he borrows from Sargent and Paraskevas.[27] In this exercise, he asks participants in the audience to freewrite on a given prompt while simultaneously doing all of the following:

- **Put an exclamation mark! after every proper noun.** If you can't remember what proper nouns are, just make your best guess.
- **Put an asterisk* by every preposition.** If you can't remember what prepositions are, again, make your best guess—but here's a short refresher course: put asterisk *above*, *below*, *in front of*, or *behind* whatever you think is a preposition.
- **CAPITALIZE every R, S, V, and B wherever they appear**—not just at the beginning of a word, but at the end of a word and also in the middle.
- **~~Delete~~ every "ing" from any word in which it appears**—not just from verb forms, as in "jumping" or "writing," but also from words like "ring" and "springing" (two cases there!)—strike out the ~~ing~~.
- **<u>Underline every adverbial phrase or clause</u>.** Again, if you've forgotten what those are, just take your best shot.

He then has participants write for a few more minutes on the same prompt without such restrictions. He asks each person to compare the amount of text they wrote under each circumstance. Inevitably, participants write more and express their thoughts more fluently without the constraints. While one may argue that these are just arbitrary rules, Hafer points out that so are the rules that govern language and grammar. This exercise clearly shows how easily working memory is overloaded when it is asked to do too many activities simultaneously and simulates the student writing process when they expect (or are expected) to produce polished, correct, and meaningful writing all at once.

Perrault blames much of the poor student writing that educators complain about on cognitive overload.[28] He says that learning does not lead to an obvious gradual improvement, either for content knowledge or learning how to write. Instead, it dips as students struggle with each significant increase in difficulty levels, leading them to commit errors in content and skills that seem quite basic to educators. Such dips are followed by leaps in ability as students master the new content, though not necessarily before the paper is due. He concludes that "improvement will come only when a reduction in cognitive overload allows the writer to allocate attention to clarity and correctness in his or her prose."[29]

Problems with cognitive overload plague both novice and experienced writers, but each group handles these problems differently. Novice writers frequently give up when they are overwhelmed. In contrast, expert writers have developed sophisticated strategies for breaking down a big task into more manageable pieces. When writing-from-sources, this means a lot of informal writing, particularly in the form of drafts, outlines, notes, and research journals. Initial drafts that focus on generating and exploring ideas are bound to be poorly written. However, once the ideas are recorded on paper or screen, they can be organized, developed, and refined through revision and rewriting and finally edited for the proper mechanics and grammar in order to be considerate of the cognitive load they place on future readers. Novice researchers, on the other hand, need help breaking down a complex writing-from-sources task.

In the traditional one-shot model of information literacy instruction, librarians can do little more than encourage students to spread the research paper out over time. However, with closer collaboration with teaching faculty, librarians can assist novice researchers in developing writing-from-sources habits that diminish the effects of cognitive overload by encouraging good assignment design, providing structured instructional support throughout the research paper process, and offering one-on-one research assistance at the reference desk that goes beyond finding sources. Any of these approaches to improving support for students' writing-from-sources papers will inevitably involve low-stakes writing activities.

One example, note-taking, is one area where librarians can develop expertise in low-stakes writing specifically for spreading out cognitive load. While students frequently write their papers directly from highlighted article print-outs, their research process could be drawn out and the cognitive load reduced if they would invest time and energy in taking notes from the information sources they used. Successful note-taking alleviates a writer's cognitive load by processing the information read from texts through paraphrasing. When one begins to write, one is not attempting to make meaning through reading and writing simultaneously, which can lead to significant cognitive overload. Note-taking also serves as external storage of information so that readers/writers do not have to remember everything they have read. Finally, it also allows readers/writers to extract specific information from sources useful to their own rhetorical goal so that they are not distracted by the remaining irrelevant information in those sources.

Nelson and Hayes found significant differences in note-taking habits between students who took high- and low-investment approaches to research assignments.[30] The students who took the low-investment approach "condens[ed] notetaking and text production into essentially one act."[31] In contrast, they noted that one of the students who adopted a high-investment approach took notes that helped her to understand the source in relation to her own information needs. Mueller and Oppenheimer found that students who took paraphrased lecture notes processed the material more deeply and significantly outperformed verbatim notetakers on conceptual questions.[32] One can logically conclude that highlighting articles alone does not allow students to properly process the information as students read from sources. If deeper processing of information from texts is left until drafting, students will be trying to accomplish too many steps of the research process at once. These two studies begin to shed light on the importance of good note-taking to spread out the cognitive load of writing-from-sources.

Many teaching faculty already break down writing-from-sources assignments into mini assignments. In a recent survey we conducted at my institution, Lycoming College, 72 percent of students said their last research assignment was broken down into steps. The most popular mini assignments included drafts, annotated bibliographies, thesis proposals, outlines, sections of the paper, and bibliographies. Teaching faculty are increasingly breaking down large writing-from-sources assignments to encourage students to prolong their learning, produce better papers, avoid plagiarism, and receive feedback from the instructor. The effectiveness of such mini assignments in promoting student success was not studied in the survey but is a topic of interest in assessments with teaching faculty. The usefulness of such assignments in spreading out students' cognitive load is most likely determined by how naturally the assignments contribute to the final product. Instruction librarians can collaborate with teaching faculty to help design effective mini assignments that use low-stakes writing to spread out the cognitive load of writing-from-sources in natural and authentic ways.

2. Making Thoughts Visible for Oneself in Order to Promote Metacognition

Another valuable aspect of informal reflective writing is that it promotes metacognition, which is the most important skill for promoting transfer of knowledge learned in one context to another.[33] Researchers at all levels of experience can come to profound realizations about the topic, roadblocks, or themselves as learners that never would have otherwise been made apparent if their thoughts had not been written down. Furthermore, metacognition helps readers/writers monitor their comprehension, distribute cognitive resources, predict and evaluate the usefulness of sources, make connections between ideas, and surmount problems in the writing-from-sources process. Metacognition is considered a late-developing skill, with only some students being metacognitively mature when they begin their undergraduate careers.[34] Like any other skill, habit, or attitude, metacognition must be actively encouraged by educators through structured reflection exercises.

Thinking in the form of written reflection enables a writer to take experience, including information obtained through reading, and transform it into knowledge and learning. Maintaining a research journal can promote reflection and metacognition, although reflective writing does not have to be as systematic as a journal. Boud points out that reflection has different purposes at the various stages of an experience.[35] When reflecting *before* an experience, one anticipates what is yet to come. Boud says one can ask oneself, "What can we do to make the most of future events?"[36] When preparing for a writing-from-sources task, students can use informal writing to audit what they know about the potential topic, what they feel about the topic and assignment, and how they understand the problem that needs to be solved. They can predict the usefulness of an information source based on its title, abstract, or table of contents in their research journal to encourage deeper critical thinking. Such anticipatory thinking can help a writer find purpose and motivation, and also it can reveal the writer's tacit assumptions, values, and beliefs that need to be consciously analyzed before they divert precious energy and cognitive resources away from fruitful pursuits.

During the experience, one becomes aware of one's own efforts and thought processes, which can improve one's overall metacognitive abilities over time. Useful low-stakes writing during the writing-from-sources experience includes making lists, clustering concepts, capturing half-baked ideas, and identifying relationships between pieces of information. It is a safe place to explore any and all ideas. Through such exploration, writers can obtain greater knowledge of themselves as learners, the task they are working on, and the various strategies they are employing to work through the activity of writing-from-sources.

When engaging in reflective writing *after* the experience, one returns to it, reevaluates the experience with the advantage of hindsight, and gets ready for the next experience. One often understands an experience better when it is over than when one is in the middle of it. However, one must make the time to reflect in order to learn as much as possible from the experience. Educators who use low-stakes writing assignments to enhance student learning can include reflections on writing-from-sources experiences *after* they are complete. These assignments should have students reflect on both the cognitive and affective aspects of the experience and encourage students to reevaluate the experience from the new perspective of having completed it.[37] If students have kept a research journal, they should be encouraged to read and respond to previous journal entries. Even without systematic journal keeping, students can be encouraged to look at the materials they used to prepare the assignment as part of their reflective process. Students should reflect on what they learned from the experience to understand what practices should be part of their next writing-from-sources assignments. Through reflective writing, educators can help students see that this is the end of one cycle and the beginning of a new one.

Opportunities for reflection can be built into the information literacy one-shot session through questions that prompt students to engage in low-stakes writing for a short amount of time. An example question could be, "Think of an area in which you are an expert. What makes you an expert? What does this tell you about expertise?" It is my experience that students will reflect more deeply and more frequently be willing to share their responses with the class when they are first given a chance to reflect in writing. The librarian can then lead a class discussion from students' responses to challenge them to further reflect as a community and to correct any misunderstandings or fill in comprehension gaps. With more collaboration with teaching faculty, librarians can help design reflective writing exercises at key points in the research process. In non–information literacy settings, I have seen students come to important realizations about their learning progress through such assignments, which they could have learned in no other way.

3. Making Thoughts Visible for Evaluation and Feedback

Undergraduates' reflective low-stakes writing is important not only for the learners themselves, but also because it makes the students' thought processes visible to educators, which then allows educators to provide students with constructive feedback. This is called formative assessment, best described as "in-the-process-of-learning assessments."[38] Instead of waiting to give written feedback only at the end of a formal writing assignment, when students least need it to further their learning, educators provide feedback on work that is still in development.[39] Feedback on low-stakes writing assignments can further critical thinking and metacognition, providing encouragement to dig deeper, redirecting students' processes when they go in unproductive directions, or offering new perspectives on issues or problems the students experience. It can help students break free from simply reprocessing the same concepts repeatedly, something inexperienced thinkers are prone to do.[40] Librarians can work with teaching faculty to design opportunities for formative assessment of informal writing. Access to these results can be obtained to have a better understanding of the decisions students make during the research process and can provide students with an additional perspective on how to progress toward the final paper.

While low-stakes writing is a critical part of the writing-from-sources process, students are unlikely to engage in it unless it there is an incentive to do so, which is often accomplished by being held accountable by an educator. Indeed, the literature acknowledges even with educator-led accountability, students may still struggle to reflect deeply enough in their reflective writing for educators to understand their thought processes or provide useful feedback.[41] Students must invest emotional and cognitive resources into reflective writing in order for it to be beneficial to either the student or educators. The literature on journals does not yet provide clear advice for creating assignments that make such reflection more likely to happen. For now, educators must experiment with reflection assignment instructions, assess, and reevaluate their future efforts based on assessment results.

Formative assessment is intended to provide students with a safe place to learn through experimentation and feedback. Educators should therefore avoid grading low-stakes writing assignments for anything other than effort. The purpose is for educators to understand student thinking and provide constructive feedback. Reflective writing is not useful to either party if students write only what they assume the educator wants to read, which is likely to occur if they expect a grade on such assignments. As Hafer points out, feedback drives learning forward, grading puts an end to it.[42]

It may sound like a burden to give such feedback, but it does not have to be. Ash, Clayton, and Atkinson use trained student "reflection leaders" to provide original feedback on students' reflective writing.[43] Hafer explains how he has successfully given students meaningful feedback without taking on an overwhelming burden by establishing daily writing among his students, but collecting only some of their low-stakes writing.[44] Of this, he makes a point of reading and responding as quickly as possible. He also uses brief in-person conferences to give oral feedback, which is faster than writing out such feedback and also keeps the responsibility for improvement with the student.

There is some literature on librarians using low-stakes writing for both formative and summative assessment. Ariew (librarian) and Van Ingen (teaching faculty) have successfully used research logs specifically to promote metacognition in the writing-from-sources process.[45] The research logs showed how students' confidence fluctuated greatly throughout the research process, they struggled to manage research questions, and their ability to reflect on their research processes varied greatly. Librarians at West Virginia University collaborated with teaching faculty and writing tutors to spread information literacy instruction over several sessions and incorporated three isolated research log assignments.[46] The librarians responded directly to the logs. They found "the process of responding to student writing also reinforces the collaborative aspect of the course because it keeps the librarians in conversation with the writing teachers and, from the students' perspective, it underscores the authority and voice that the librarians have as part of the instructional team."[47] In another example from the LIS literature, Isbell and Broaddus describe a class that was equally cotaught by a member of the teaching faculty and a librarian.[48] They both provided feedback on student work, as well as facilitated peers providing feedback to each other on low-stakes writing. Other examples of reflective writing assignments that promote educators' ability to assess students' information literacy skills include annotated bibliographies, mind maps, guided research templates, and elaborations on or responses to questions on texts used for research. If such mini assignments are built into a writing-from-sources project, librarians can ask to be involved in evaluating and providing feedback as much as possible.

4. Possible Key to Motivation

Professional writers often talk about launching into a new research project driven by a strong desire to solve a question or problem. Bean talks about writers experiencing cognitive dissonance, saying that a "writer-to-be" finds the current conversation on a topic "somehow unsatisfactory; something is missing, wrongheaded, unexplained, or otherwise puzzling."[49] Leist writes something similar when she says, "When a working academic starts a research project, that project is usually involved with some aspect of his or her professional existence which has caused the person to be disturbed in some way."[50] This cognitive dissonance leads to intense motivation to resolve an uncomfortable mental state. It "propels writers through the writing process."[51]

If one of the purposes of writing-from-sources assignments is to move students from novice to experienced practitioners in the discipline, it is important to look at what sparks cognitive dissonance in the discipline's professionals and learn how to develop an equivalent in students. One of the differences between these two groups is the level of disciplinary critical thinking they engage in. The cognitive dissonance described above happens at very high levels of critical thinking, which few undergraduates initially practice without assistance for academic topics. Curiosity needs to be developed and encouraged. Low-stakes writing can be an important tool for enhancing curiosity because it can bring out questions students want to answer that may otherwise lie dormant. Low-stakes writing not only shows students' thought processes after they have occurred, but also encourages those thought processes to go further. This can help students look at a topic in a new way and challenge assumptions, the dominant culture, or tacit beliefs. Therefore, low-stakes writing can help students discover topics about which they are motivated to learn.

In a recent student survey I conducted, I asked students to think about a research assignment that excited them and to explain what made them excited. The overwhelming majority said it was a topic that they were interested in, often one that they chose. There were many reasons their topic interested them, such as relation to their chosen field of study or personal history, they liked the class, they already had some background knowledge on the topic, or they were learning about something they previously knew nothing about. It was clear in many of these answers their excitement made them work much harder and think more critically on that project. Librarians should be concerned with helping students experience and be excited by curiosity to fuel their motivation so that they will be more likely to adopt high-investment approaches to writing-from-sources assignments. As low-stakes writing can help all writers think more deeply than they would otherwise, low-stakes writing can be an important tool for librarians to help foster this curiosity and motivation.

Conclusion

Students and educators alike tend to take low-stakes writing for granted. Yet it plays a critical role in both the writing and learning process when writing-from-sources. Students who are encouraged to spend time with low-stakes writing are more likely to spread out the cognitive load of large writing-from-sources assignments, think more critically, have more opportunities for educator and peer feedback during the process, and develop curiosity and motivation for their topics. Chapter 4 will explore how low-stakes writing assignments can enhance students' understanding of their information texts. Chapter 5 will examine how low-stakes writing can contribute to improved synthesis of information from multiple sources and to high-stakes writing through mid-stakes drafts. Experienced writers and researchers engage in these forms of low-stakes writing, so assigning them instills good habits among novice researchers.

Low-stakes writing equally benefits educators as it is a tool to focus on the research process, where student learning in writing-from-sources assignments occurs. It creates artifacts of student thinking that allow educators to see into students' thought processes and better understand their decisions. Furthermore, educators can provide feedback on these artifacts to encourage critical thinking and ensure students are progressing in their learning. Because it plays such an important role in learning, librarians can use short reflective writing assignments in the traditional information literacy session. However, they can also collaborate with teaching faculty to design and assess low-stakes writing assignments throughout the writing-from-sources process.

Notes

1.   John C. Bean, *Engaging Ideas: The Professor's Guide to Integrating Writing, Critical Thinking, and Active Learning in the Classroom* (San Francisco: Jossey-Bass, 1996), 16.

2. Elaine P. Maimon, Barbara F. Nodine, and Finbarr W. O'Connor, *Thinking, Reasoning, and Writing* (New York: Longman, 1989); Richard Menary, "Writing as Thinking," *Language Sciences* 29, no. 5 (2007): 621–32; Donald Morison Murray, *A Writer Teaches Writing: A Practical Method of Teaching Composition*, 2nd ed. (Boston: Houghton Mifflin, 1985).

3. Kate Koppelman, "Literary Eavesdropping and the Socially Graceful Critic," in *Teaching Literary Research: Challenges in a Changing Environment*, ed. Kathleen A. Johnson and Steven R. Harris (Chicago: Association of College and Research Libraries, 2009), 42.

4. Kacy Lundstrom, Anne R. Diekema, Heather Leary, Sheri Haderlie, and Wendy Holliday, "Teaching and Learning Information Synthesis," *Communications in Information Literacy* 9, no. 1 (2015): 60–82; Wendy Holliday, Betty Dance, Erin Davis, Britt Fagerheim, Anne Hedrich, Kacy Lundstrom, and Pamela Martin, "An Information Literacy Snapshot: Authentic Assessment across the Curriculum," *College and Research Libraries* 76, no. 2 (2015): 170–87.

5. Gary R. Hafer, *Embracing Writing: Ways to Teach Reluctant Writers in Any College Course* (San Francisco: Jossey-Bass, 2014).

6. Ibid., 19.

7. Ronald Thomas Kellogg, *The Psychology of Writing* (New York: Oxford University Press, 1994).

8. Lorin W. Anderson and David R. Krathwohl, *A Taxonomy for Learning, Teaching, and Assessing: A Revision of Bloom's Taxonomy of Educational Objectives* (New York: Longman, 2001).

9. Margaret A. Boden, "Creativity as a Neuroscientific Mystery," in *Neuroscience of Creativity*, ed. Oshin Vartanian, Adam S. Bristol, and James C. Kaufman (Cambridge, MA: MIT Press, 2013), 3.

10. Hafer, *Embracing Writing*.

11. Ibid.

12. Peter Elbow, *Vernacular Eloquence: What Speech Can Bring to Writing* (Oxford: Oxford University Press, 2012).

13. Peter Elbow, *Everyone Can Write: Essays toward a Hopeful Theory of Writing and Teaching Writing* (New York: Oxford University Press, 2000), 41.

14. Linda Flower, *Problem-Solving Strategies for Writing*, 4th ed. (New York: Harcourt Brace Jovanovich, 1993), 5.

15. Hafer, *Embracing Writing*.

16. Toby Fulwiler, ed., *The Journal Book* (Portsmouth, NH: Boynton/Cook), 1.

17. Toby Fulwiler, *College Writing: A Personal Approach to Academic Writing* (Portsmouth, NH: Boynton/Cook, 1997).

18. Mary Broussard and Gary R. Hafer, "Write Away: Ways to Kickstart Writing from Your Desk to Your Class" (presentation, Lycoming College Teaching Effectiveness Luncheon, Williamsport, PA, February 17, 2015).

19. Mike Rohde, *The Sketchnote Handbook: The Illustrated Guide to Visual Note Taking* (San Francisco: Peachpit Press, 2013), 2.

20. Ibid., 10.

21. Daniel J. Levitin, *The Organized Mind: Thinking Straight in the Age of Information Overload* (New York: Dutton, 2014).

22. John C. Bean in discussion with the author, August 2015.

23. David Boud, "Using Journal Writing to Enhance Reflective Practice," *New Directions for Adult and Continuing Education 2001*, no. 90 (2001): 9.

24. Marsha C. Lovett, "Make Exams Worth More Than the Grade: Using Exam Wrappers to Promote Metacognition," in *Using Reflection and Metacognition to Improve Student Learning: Across the Disciplines, Across the Academy*, ed. Matthew Kaplan, Naomi Sliver, Danielle LaVaque-Manty, and Deborah Meizlish (Sterling, VA: Stylus, 2013), 18–52.

25. Fulwiler, *The Journal Book.*

26. Kellogg, *The Psychology of Writing*, 150.

27. M. Elizabeth Sargent and Cornelia C. Paraskevas, eds., *Conversations about Writing: Eavesdropping, Inkshedding, and Joining In* (Toronto: Nelson, 2005).

28. S. T. Perrault, "Cognition and Error in Student Writing," *Journal on Excellence in College Teaching* 22, no. 3 (2011): 51.

29. Ibid., 52–53.

30. Jennie Nelson and John R. Hayes, *How the Writing Context Shapes College Students' Strategies for Writing from Sources* (Berkeley, CA: Center for the Study of Writing, Carnegie Mellon University, 1988).

31. Ibid., 9.

32. Pam A. Mueller and Daniel M. Oppenheimer, "The Pen Is Mightier Than the Keyboard: Advantages of Longhand over Laptop Note Taking," *Psychological Science* 25, no. 6 (2014): 1159–68.

33. Ruth Benander and Robin Lightner, "Promoting Transfer of Learning: Connecting General Education Courses," *Journal of General Education* 54, no. 3 (2005), 199–208.

34. Priscilla L. Griffith and Jiening Raun, "What Is Metacognition and What Should Be Its Role in Literacy Instruction?" in *Metacognition in Literacy Learning: Theory, Assessment, Instruction, and Professional Development*, ed. Susan E. Israel, Cathy Collins Block, Kathryn L. Bauserman, and Kathryn Kinnucan-Welsch (Mahwah, NJ: L. Erlbaum Associates, 2005), 3–18.

35. Boud, "Using Journal Writing."

36. Ibid., 12.

37. Ibid.

38. Eva L. Baker and Girly C. Delacruz, "Framework for the Assessment of Learning in Games," in *Computer Games and Team and Individual Learning*, ed. Harold F. O'Neil and Ray S. Perez (London: Elsevier, 2007), 21–37.

39. Hafer, *Embracing Writing.*

40. Ibid.

41. Timothy O'Connell and Janet Dyment, "Reflections on Using Journals in Higher Education: A Focus Group Discussion with Faculty," *Assessment and Evaluation in Higher Education* 31, no. 6 (2006): 678; Janet E. Dyment and Timothy S. O'Connell, "Assessing the Quality of Reflection in Student Journals: A Review of the Research," *Teaching in Higher Education* 16, no. 1 (2011): 81–97

42. Hafer, *Embracing Writing.*

43. Sarah L. Ash, Patti H. Clayton, and Maxine P. Atkinson, "Integrating Reflection and Assessment to Capture and Improve Student Learning," *Michigan Journal of Community Service Learning* 11, no. 2 (2005): 49–60.

44. Hafer, *Embracing Writing.*

45. Susan A. Ariew and Sarah Van Ingen, "Making the Invisible Visible," accessed May

20, 2016, https://works.bepress.com/susan_ariew/25/.

46. Laura Brady, Nathalie Singh-Corcoran, Jo Ann Dadisman, and Kelly Diamond, "A Collaborative Approach to Information Literacy: First-Year Composition, Writing Center, and Library Partnerships at West Virginia University," *Composition Forum* 19 (Spring 2009), http://compositionforum.com/issue/19/west-virginia.php.

47. Ibid.

48. Dennis Isbell and Dorothy Broaddus, "Teaching Writing and Research as Inseparable: A Faculty-Librarian Teaching Team," *Reference Services Review* 23, no. 4 (1995): 51–62.

49. Bean, *Engaging Ideas*, 30.

50. Susan R. Mondschein Leist, *Writing to Teach; Writing to Learn in Higher Education* (Lanham, MD: University Press of America, 2006), 83.

51. Bean, *Engaging Ideas*, 31.

CHAPTER 4

Reading for Comprehension and Reading to Write

A text, once it leaves its author's hands, is simply paper and
ink until a reader evokes from it a literary work.

—Rosenblatt[1]

A cademic librarians generally focus on a very small part of the research
process, with a particular focus on *finding* information, citation, and
perhaps superficial treatment of information evaluation and plagiarism. Fister fears that "teaching library research as information retrieval
through tools valorizes information retrieval as the purpose of research,"[2] a
sentiment others echo.[3] As Friedman and Miller point out, because "finding
the source is really only the beginning of the process from the student's point
of view,"[4] librarians should not limit themselves to teaching information access
alone. Reading comprehension skills are an essential part of using information, yet research repeatedly shows nearly all undergraduates need additional
support in reading comprehension skills than are typically received in American institutions of higher education. While the *Framework* has very little that
directly addresses reading comprehension, it is an assumed skill required by
all of the frames. As shall be explored in this chapter, source evaluation as presented in the *Framework* cannot be separated from reading comprehension.

At the very least, librarians need to be aware of how complex meaning
making through reading truly is and present it as such when they teach.
A handful of LIS authors make an argument for stronger involvement in

improving students' reading abilities. Cunningham and Hannon felt responsible for teaching students to read scholarly articles when they realized students were avoiding harder, more appropriate texts in favor of ones they could more easily understand.[5] Moreillon, coming from a secondary school perspective, argues that reading is so intertwined with teaching students to become "effective users of ideas and information" that school media specialists should collaborate with other educators to support reading comprehension.[6] Simmons argues that "helping students to examine and question the social, economic, and political context for the production and consumption of information is a vital corollary to teaching the skills of information literacy."[7] MacMillan and Rosenblatt make the argument that best mirrors the one in this chapter, which is, "Helping students interpret scholarly sources is a natural extension of our work as librarians. It should be incorporated into our understanding of information literacy."[8] Both MacMillan and Rosenblatt's and Simmons's articles argue that it is precisely because librarians move between academic disciplines that they are best able to bridge the gap between the faculty who have been entrenched in the disciplinary literature for years and the students who have never seen it before. Both also argue that the responsibility for teaching these skills must be shared with teaching faculty.

The literature on students' reading skills is overwhelmingly focused on elementary school students *learning to read*. By late elementary school, young students become proficient *decoders*, meaning they can effectively translate written symbols into ideas. At this point, where instruction should be shifting from *learning to read* to developing *reading comprehension skills*, formal education in the United States tends to stop providing explicit reading instruction and instead leaves students to figure this out on their own.[9] Perhaps this is why so many studies find high school and college students' reading skills less than satisfactory. The 2013 National Assessment of Educational Progress (NAEP) revealed that only 38 percent of 12th graders are reading at or above the proficient level, with even poorer scores among several minority groups and in certain geographic locations.[10] Schoenbach and colleagues observe that high school teachers frequently react to poor reading skills by reducing reading assignments, a trend that Lei and colleagues say continues through college.[11] Wentzell, Richlin, and Cox, editors of *The Journal on Excellence in College Teaching*, say that they are frequently contacted by professors who say their students do not read effectively.[12]

Several studies on students' research processes found evidence that undergraduate students' poorly written research papers were a direct result of inadequate reading comprehension skills. Howard, Serviss, and Rodrigue concluded that students' patchwriting and poor paraphrasing (both frequently considered plagiarism) indicated that students were reading only small parts of the sources they cited and demonstrated only a superficial understanding of the texts' meaning.[13] In the LIS literature, a recent study conducted by Holliday and colleagues found that "students struggled most in categories that required critical thinking, including evaluating information, synthesizing information, and using information effectively in their writing."[14] These studies show that students are struggling to understand the texts they are reading for research assignments.

While teaching faculty in higher education frequently blame students' inability to read and write on high school teachers, both teaching faculty and academic librarians must also recognize that a significant part of the reading comprehension problem among undergraduates is due to the *types* of texts students are asked to read in order to write college-level research papers. The literature on high school reading indicates that students' experiences with texts are mainly limited to textbooks and fiction.[15] A local survey I recently conducted on my campus found many students had little experience with writing-from-sources in high school, frequently saying the papers they were assigned were primarily based on their own opinions. The reading literature stresses that expertise in one domain of reading does not automatically transfer to another.[16] If students have not had experiences with scholarly texts before arriving at college, they need explicit support in comprehending them.

In addition to undergraduates' inexperience with scholarly texts, it is important to remember that these texts were written for an audience of other academics who have a great deal of background knowledge on the subject to help with comprehension of new information. Undergraduate students are *not* the intended audience for whom scholarly articles are written. However, meaningful interactions with these texts are critical for students to become acculturated into the language and practice of the discipline. Students need help as they begin *actively* looking in on the scholarly discussions represented in these texts, comprehending as much as possible even when they are outsiders. Such assistance should continue as they gradually develop discipline-specific background knowledge and advanced reading skills over their college careers.

Fortunately, the research on reading comprehension among high school and college students agrees that it is never too late to improve students' reading comprehension skills. In fact, Wolf writes, "The end of reading development doesn't exist."[17] Everyone can continue to develop their reading skills. Students come to college with a wide variety of reading comprehension experience levels, with some students needing more basic help than others. Librarians can work with teaching faculty to come to a solid understanding of the reading skills and experiences their students bring to college, then help design explicit instruction to help students transition to the academic texts with which they are required to engage in order to write from sources.

Meaning Making from Texts

In their argument for a rhetoricized information literacy, Bowles-Terry, Davis, and Holliday argue that student's "cut-and-paste" attitude toward information comes from outdated behavioralist views of pedagogy in which "learning is based on precise, well-defined, and measurable behaviors and rules."[18] Simmons argues that the *Standards'* "approach to information literacy seems based on a positivist epistemology in which seekers can discover a unified 'Truth,' even though knowledge is dispersed and decentralized in our current postmodern information environment."[19] The critique that current views of information literacy are based on outmoded pedagogies and undemocratic ideologies is echoed elsewhere in the literature on critical information literacy, where librarians are dedicated to challenging the illusion that information is neutral and without context and that students are blank slates who bring nothing to the research experience.[20]

Current theories of information literacy pedagogy, as can be seen in the *Framework*, emphasize a constructivist approach in which educators value students' prior knowledge. New knowledge can be constructed only by building onto what they already know. Scholars agree that reading is a complex activity that is commonly misunderstood, frequently to the detriment of student learning. Instead of a passive activity, it is a complex and creative *interaction* with a text. A person's background knowledge and goal for reading deeply influence the meaning that is made, and that meaning will be unique to a particular reader at a particular point in time. It is important for educators to understand how people learn through reading so that they can support students' development in this area as the reading of texts (along with other informational sources) is the basis of so much learning in our current society.

There are many types of reading. While they are all related, this chapter focuses specifically on the kind that is relevant to academic librarians: *efferent* reading. Rosenblatt distinguished *efferent* reading, meaning reading to become informed, from *aesthetic* reading, which is reading for the experience.[21] In efferent reading, she says that the "primary concern of the reader is with what he will carry away from the reading,"[22] explaining that she chose this word as it comes from the Latin word *efferre*, which means "to carry away." Though they do not use the term *efferent reading*, Adler and Van Doren also focus on this type of reading, saying the reason one reads a text is because the reader wants to know something the author knows, and through the reading exchange, an active reader gradually becomes the equal of the author on the subject at hand.[23] Expert researchers read efferent texts with a particular goal in mind, which strongly affects how they go about making meaning from the text because it draws their attention to the specific parts of the texts that will help them attain their goals. In short, efferent reading is goal-directed reading. Novice researchers need explicit guidance on how to use their goal to read their texts effectively.

The act of reading is an extremely interactive and complex process with both social (interpersonal) and cognitive (intrapersonal) aspects. Reading is social because the reader is engaging with the mind and worldview of the text's author.[24] In order to transmit meaning through reading a text, the author and reader work together to make meaning. As written by the author, the text narrows down the possible meanings readers can make from it, but the readers—each with a unique combination of background knowledge, previous experiences, values, beliefs, and goals for reading—will always bring a degree of creativity to the reading event.[25] Reading is also an extremely cognitive, *intra*personal activity involving critical thinking and problem solving, one in which the reader must make an infinite number of mostly unconscious decisions that enable him or her to extrapolate meaning from the text.

Making meaning from a text requires the brain to not only connect individual words but also to connect their meaning to what the brain already knows. Information is more useful for comprehension and retrieval if it is meaningfully grouped. Such groupings of similar information in the brain are called *schemata* (singular *schema*), which have been briefly introduced in previous chapters but will be further explored in this one. Rumelhart and Ortony call schemata the "basic building blocks of the human information-processing system."[26] To any reading event, a reader brings a lifetime of knowledge, experience, beliefs, and emotions in the form of schemata. Brent stresses that schemata "do not force a particular interpretation. Rather, they are tentative estimates of significance, tried on for size and then abandoned in favor of a better whenever necessary."[27] In other words, schemata are flexible and frequently changing (although mostly in small ways) knowledge structures.

Schemata serve two purposes. The first is to allow a reader to make important inferences about a text's meaning, what is frequently referred to as *reading between the lines*. Anderson and colleagues give a number of examples, such as what the word *kick* means in the following sentences:

> The baby kicked the ball.
> The punter kicked the ball.
> The golfer kicked the ball.[28]

What the reader knows about babies, punters, and golfers affects how a reader interprets each sentence. The baby is likely to have accidentally kicked the ball, and it likely did not go far. A punter is a position in football, likely a man who is highly skilled at kicking the ball a very long distance. As golfers do not normally kick a ball, it is logical to infer that the golfer is angry. All readers make such inferences constantly and almost entirely unconsciously, and these inferences greatly influence the meaning extracted from a text. Because such inferences are extremely important for understanding and evaluating texts, novice readers are likely to need help making those inferences conscious and explicit so they can have control of them.

The second purpose of schemata is to serve as a foundation on which to evaluate new information and build new knowledge. Brent argues that if one views reading as looking for information to absorb into one's own worldview, then it is particularly important to evaluate such information and its source.[29] With the wealth of information available, information evaluation is a key skill in helping a reader to decide what to believe and what not to believe. The importance of evaluation is widely accepted by educators, but it is commonly taught to students with checklist methods such as CRITIC and CRAAP, which Radom and Gammons call oversimplified, linear, mechanical, and algorithmic.[30] The literature on rhetorical reading presents a much richer and more complex view of evaluating texts in which evaluation and comprehension are inextricably intertwined.[31]

There are at least two major overlapping models of rhetorical approaches to information evaluation. The first is analyzing how the purpose, audience, and genre of a text relate to one's own purpose for reading. This is what Bean, Chappell, and Gillam call *rhetorical reading*[32] and Adler and Van Doren call *syntopical reading*.[33] In rhetorical/syntopical reading, readers are always looking for connections between authors' intended meanings and their own rhetorical goals, which may be very different. Students are very likely to need help through modeling and guiding questions given to them by educators until they have developed skills to independently question an author's purpose, audience, and genre along with an ability to connect authors' goals and meanings to their own rhetorical purposes.

The second model of efferent text evaluation is investigating the logos, ethos, and pathos of a text. These three methods of evaluation originated in ancient Greece, which was an oratory society. However, Brent elaborates on each of these as they apply to written communication.[34] Logos, or logic, includes appeals to reason. It requires the reader to analyze how effectively a text's author uses reasoning and evidence to construct claims and arguments. Pathos, or emotion, plays a role even in "objective" scholarly texts. Pathos involves the values and beliefs of both the writer and the reader. Brent argues that emotions are "a valid source of evidence for knowing."[35] An author's emotional evidence can have as powerful an effect on convincing a reader as logical evidence. Furthermore, readers' combinations of fuzzy, unstable beliefs and values affect how they make meaning from texts and what they choose to incorporate into their own worldviews. In the modern text-driven society, the reader must evaluate the ethos, or credibility, of a text's author in his or her absence. While textually external clues remain important to information evaluation, such as an author's education and reputation, educators must also teach students to look for more subtle clues of credibility within the text, such as choice of words and arguments. Indeed, information evaluation that takes logos, pathos, and ethos into consideration will require a good deal of critical thinking on the part of the reader.

In each of these models, readers use their background knowledge, values, beliefs, experiences, goals, and specific evaluation and comprehension strategies to decide which ideas to assimilate (absorb) into existing schemata, what information will require one's schemata to change (accommodation), and what information they will reject as implausible.[36] This is not all or nothing; readers can decide what and with what intensity to believe. Too much rejection or doubt will lead to a failure to learn, while too much acceptance will lead to mental anarchy.[37] Any reader will need to assimilate and accommodate in order to learn.

Reading and the *Framework*

The *Framework* never once mentions the word *read* or *reading* except in the context of educators and administrators reading the *Framework* itself. However, rhetorical reading undergirds the entire document. The *Framework* emphasizes the importance of "reflective discovery of information" as well as the context of texts' creation that both imply deep, critical readings of efferent texts. Furthermore, evaluation is one of the most frequent themes in the *Framework*, which encourages librarians to teach how to evaluate not only a text's quality—what Rouet and colleagues call "reasoning *about* documents"[38]—but also the text's potential ability to meet one's goal for efferent reading in a writing-from-sources context, which will lead to one's ability to reason *with* documents.

Many LIS authors, the *Framework*, and composition and rhetoric theory challenge librarians and teaching faculty to present students with a richer concept of source evaluation than the commonly taught checklist methods.[39] Coming from a rhetorical perspective, one cannot separate evaluation and reading comprehension. A reader must understand a text in order to evaluate its quality or relevance. While old concepts of evaluation, such as an author's credentials, still play a role in information evaluation, such criteria only *predict* the usefulness of the source. Students must actually *read* a text in order to evaluate it, which is admittedly a challenge when teaching evaluation in the one-shot session. Under the "Authority Is Constructed and Contextual" frame, the *Framework* acknowledges that "novice learners may need to rely on basic indicators of authority, such as type of publication or author credentials," but that is not what educators should present as the epitome of what students should know about and be able to do in regard to information evaluation. Librarians rarely teach evaluation in terms of determining relevance or knowing when one has enough information to complete the information task. However, it is a critical aspect of information literacy. As Bowles-Terry, Davis, and Holliday argue, "Evaluating information is a key component of IL and writing. As such, it is a shared learning goal for librarians and writing instructors,"[40] or any teaching faculty who assign writing-from-sources assignments.

The *Framework* also stresses the importance of understanding the sociocultural contexts in which texts were created. This is particularly evident in the "Information Creation as a Process" frame, but it is present in all of the frames. This means readers must analyze the imagined situation and process of the published authors of the texts they read to truly understand and use the information the texts present. Brent writes, "We can not only look at why a particular author phrases her arguments in just such a way; we can also inquire into the development of the ideas themselves."[41] Looking at the thinking processes of published experts enables students to become better thinkers and writers within the discipline themselves.[42] Burkholder encourages looking at sources as social acts.[43] He writes, "Sources—from personal blogs to television news stories to scientific journal articles—are different, because they address different rhetorical situations."[44] He argues that instead of simply being taught that library sources are *better* than free Internet resources, students should be taught to analyze the context in which different sources were written and how those contexts shape the traits of those sources and how they can be used.

Finally, three of the six frames, "Information Creation as a Process," "Research as Inquiry," and "Searching as Strategic Exploration," stress the messy, iterative nature of research, where reflection, reading, and writing happen simultaneously throughout the knowledge-creation and meaning-making process. In effective research processes, students do not simply read, then write their own drafts. Instead, they are reflective, comparing texts to their background knowledge, figuring out how conflicting ideas fit together, and intentionally seeking multiple perspectives. This happens over time. Students will go back and forth between reading and the various types of low-stakes writing described in the previous chapter.

A thorough rhetorical approach to the *Framework* requires that students be taught both theoretical knowledge of reading and practical reading comprehension strategies in order to overcome the all-too-common comprehension problems for both single texts and syntheses of multiple texts. All six frames require deep, analytical, and critical reading skills that often are taken for granted by American institutions of higher education, which tend to focus exclusively on remedial writing and math skills to the detriment of reading skills. This, combined with the arguments throughout this book that information literacy involves not just finding information but actually understanding and *using* information effectively, is powerful evidence that librarians should explore ways to ensure students receive the reading comprehension support they need. By providing this support, librarians will ensure student success in information use as part of engaging in the writing-from-sources process in college and beyond.

Reading Comprehension Strategies to Teach Students

Given how foundational reading is to information literacy, librarians should seriously consider joining teaching faculty in taking responsibility for teaching reading comprehension through specific strategies based on constructivist pedagogies. As Bowles-Terry, Davis, and Holliday point out, constructivist approaches to education "emphasiz[e]… strategies rather than mechanical procedures and rules."[45] Readers need diverse reading comprehension strategies for overcoming the various reading difficulties they will encounter. This is what Schoenbach and colleagues have called a "mental toolbelt" for both understanding and evaluating individual texts, which can be another key factor in promoting transfer when combined with metacognition.[46]

In this section, each strategy will contain an introduction and description. In order to learn these strategies well enough to complete them independently, students must be explicitly taught and be given supervised opportunities to practice over time. Because low-stakes writing is such a practical tool for staying on task and making one's thoughts clear, each strategy will include an example low-stakes writing assignment. These assignments will be useful not only for the student, but also as formative assessment tools that will allow learners and educators to communicate in order to further the development of effective reading comprehension and text evaluation.

1. Questioning

Questioning is probably the most flexible strategy for reading comprehension and is an integral part of most of the other strategies listed in this chapter. Moreillon points out that this strategy helps students develop a habit of inquiry when reading. She goes on to write, "Asking and answering questions before, during, and after reading helps readers establish, develop, and maintain an internal conversation while engaging with texts or pursuing an inquiry process."[47] In other words, questions promote critical thinking among readers. Different types of questions facilitate various levels of comprehension and evaluation. Questions can start with the obvious, such as "What is this text about?" However, they should not remain limited to the superficial. Both Moreillon and Bean, Chappell, and Gillam provide a number of questions throughout their books that educators can use to get started in writing their own question-based reading assignments.[48]

During the reading and rereading of a text, readers should question the purpose of the text, its language, its creation context, and what methods of persuasion are being used. Furthermore, questions can help readers distinguish between opinion and fact and reveal assumptions within the text or within themselves. In figure 4.1 are some basic questions from Bean, Chappell, and Gillam to guide readers (both novices and experts) in reading their texts rhetorically.[49] Using such questions to guide students in creating annotated bibliographies, reading journals, or reading responses may be a useful tool in leading to more critical thinking in the writing-from-sources process, which will undoubtedly also be evident in the writing-from-sources product.

Questions for Reading Rhetorically
1. What questions does the text address? (Why are these significant questions? What community cares about them?)
2. Who is the intended audience? (Am I part of this audience or an outsider?)
3. How does the author support his or her thesis with reasons and evidence? (Do I find this argument convincing? What views and counterarguments are omitted from the text? What counterevidence is ignored?)
4. How does the author hook the intended reader's interest and keep the reader reading? (Do these appeals work for me?)
5. How does the author make himself or herself seem credible to the intended audience? (Is the author credible for me? Are the author's sources reliable?)
6. Are this writer's basic values, beliefs, and assumptions similar to or different from my own? (How does this writer's worldview accord with mine?)
7. How do I respond to this text? (Will I go along with or challenge what this text is presenting? How has it changed my thinking?)
8. How do this author's evident purposes for writing fit with my purposes for reading? (How will I be able to use what I have learned from the text?)

FIGURE 4.1
Sample activity for questioning

2. Activating Background Knowledge

As explained previously in this chapter, connecting new information to existing schemata is critical for processing information obtained through reading. New information must be incorporated into what is already known in order for it to be useful. Readers must also analyze assumptions and ideologies that prevent comprehension. While expert scholars tend to research areas in which they have significant background knowledge, novices are likely to need help in tying new information into what they already know.

Many authors who are conscientious toward their readers tap into the comprehension-assisting power of analogies, metaphors, and similes to help trigger readers' background knowledge and help them understand the new message. Grothe provides an example from Antisthenes, who says, "As iron is eaten away by rust, so the envious are consumed by their own passion."[50] Grothe elaborates,

Rather than simply assert that envy is a destructive passion, Antisthenes begins by taking a phenomenon that is well known—the damaging effect of rust on iron—and relates it to something not so familiar—the damaging effect of envy on people. By expressing his thought in an analogy, he made it very easy for people to forge a mental picture of the slow, corrosive process where-by one thing gradually eats away and eventually destroys something else.[51]

While scholarly writing is likely to contain fewer analogies, metaphors, and similes than other types of texts, when they are found they can be extremely useful for comprehension. I recently came across the following simile in a book on interpersonal communication: "Rapport is like money: it increases in importance when you do not have it, and when you do have it, a lot of opportunities appear."[52] Connecting an unfamiliar concept (rapport) to a very familiar one (money) helps readers understand the point the author is trying to make about the value of rapport. Helping students identify and take advantage of these signals is one strategy for triggering background knowledge in order to integrate new information into old. If the text does not include any analogies, metaphors, or similes, students should be encouraged to make their own to aid in comprehension, either in words when they paraphrase what they understand, or by drawing representations of their understanding.

Graphic organizers can also be useful tools in helping students connect information from readings into their existing schemata. Moreillon suggests KWL (**K**now, **W**ant to know, and **L**earn) charts to help students assess their own background knowledge.[53] Keene and Zimmermann suggest Before, During, and After questions.[54] These two very similar activities tap into the power of the questioning and predicting strategies to activate previous knowledge, get students to focus on their own goals during reading, and reflect on what they have learned in relation to that goal. Students can complete one of these for each of the texts they read in order to write their research paper (see figure 4.2).

Another way to activate background knowledge is through *elaboration*, which Stein defines as "importation of prior knowledge during information processing" by writing *any* thoughts that came to mind in the margins of a text being read (though of course not in library books).[55] These thoughts can be questions or comments that relate the content of the texts to past experiences, beliefs, or previously learned information. Stein and her colleagues found that students elaborated abundantly as they read, but much of that information was lost before the students began to write. While Stein and her colleagues used this methodology as part of a research study, it is a good strategy to encourage students to make their thought processes visible as they read. Such information can not only encourage students to think about how this new information relates to their existing schemata, it can also help them read *beyond* the text, an important step in using information rhetorically.

KWL Chart		
Complete this chart for *each of the sources you look at* in the process of writing your research paper. Begin by looking at the title and abstract (for articles) or any information given in the online catalog or on the book cover that will help you get an idea of what the text is about.		
What I Know	*What I Want to Know*	**What I Learned**
BEFORE you read the full article or book, read and think about the title and any preview information provided. What do you already know about this topic?	BEFORE you read the article, what do you hope to gain from reading this text that will help you write your paper?	DURING and AFTER you have read (and perhaps reread) the text, what are some of the facts, ideas, or arguments that will help you write your paper? Did this source meet your information need? Are there any questions you still have?

FIGURE 4.2
Sample activity for activating background knowledge

3. Using Sensory Images

Morellion explains how important sensory images are to connecting new information to relevant schemata.[56] While most of her chapter describes this strategy as being relevant to understanding literature, she does explicitly say it can also be used for informational reading as well. She admits that "for linguistic-focused educators, unpacking the meaning in other formats can be challenging."[57] Visual representations seem to be the most useful sensory image for efferent reading.

Figure 4.3 is an example of one of my own mind maps, used to cope with information overload after reading my colleague's book *Embracing Writing*.[58] Some of the visual analogies and metaphors came directly from the text, such as the analogy created between informal writing (whose value is not widely accepted) and baseball practice (which should be a familiar concept to nearly any reader). Others, such as the rope bridge representing low-stakes writing helping the stick figure reach its goal of a well-written paper, were entirely of my own invention abstractly based on the content of the text. I have found that turning complex information into representational images and arranging ideas spatially helps me identify the main ideas and their relationships between each other and has even helped me understand texts I did not previously understand.

FIGURE 4.3
Mind map created to understand Hafer's *Embracing Writing*

Using mind mapping as a reading comprehension strategy is only one of its many potential uses. I have just begun trying to teach mind mapping to students. It is important to emphasize from the very beginning that anyone can use the most basic shapes to create almost any object both they and others will recognize. Many students may need to get over embarrassment about their lack of drawing skills. Others who are visually oriented may find this to be an important step in processing information from the texts they read. Additionally, while this strategy *may* be more useful to students who have visual learning preferences, mind maps do not have to include drawings. Simply by using words and colors, readers can take advantage of the physical space on paper to represent main ideas and relationships of the texts they read that may otherwise go unnoticed.

4. Predicting

Of the reading strategies discussed thus far, predicting may be of most interest to librarians. It is the most relevant strategy for searching databases and making initial judgments of quality and relevance when attempting to determine which texts are worth one's extremely limited time and cognitive resources. While educators encourage students to read the abstracts available in article databases, they tend to treat the making of meaning from abstracts and making connections to one's own rhetorical purpose as something that students can easily figure out on their own. Yet these are sophisticated skills that deserve more attention, particularly from librarians.

Carey reports that taking a pretest on a subject before any instruction has occurred (such as through reading) generally improves learning because it gives "a detailed, specific preview of how we should begin to think about approaching a topic."[59] Laborde agrees, in the context of interpersonal communication, that since one cannot pay attention to everything all at once, it is important to direct one's limited attention to one's goals.[60] Students writing research papers should be taught to use low-stakes writing to define what kind of information they are looking for. Low-stakes writing can encourage more explicit metacognition as they analyze texts' clues in order to determine whether a further investigation will help them meet their goals. Witek developed a database-searching activity for freshmen that encourages reflection throughout the source-finding process.[61] For each *potential* source she asked students to list, she asked them to reflect on how they imagine it will be useful to answering their research question. She collected and evaluated students' responses and was pleased overall with the quality of their reflections.

Part of learning to predict the utility of a text involves learning to read texts at different speeds for different purposes. Expert readers will read titles in a database or catalog quickly until they come across one that sounds potentially useful, then more carefully analyze abstracts, if available, for these potentially relevant texts. They will next scan the text itself to determine if it merits a slower, more committed reading. Adler and Van Doren call the fast, preview stage *inspectional reading*.[62] Being able to speed read with an eye out for clues about the text's utility is an important skill in text evaluation and also an important time-management skill related to the writing-from-sources process.

A colleague in the history department has been teaching prediction to his students not only for the primary sources his discipline uses but also for secondary sources. Before beginning each new required text in his freshman seminar, he spends an entire class period asking students to predict the content of the book. They begin by looking at the title and cover, taking a moment to reflect on their predictions about the content. Then they look at the index and modify their predictions, later reading the subheadings of chapters to predict the content of the individual chapters (see figure 4.4). Even though this takes a significant amount of class time (as there are five required texts for the course), he has found the subsequent class discussions to be of a much greater quality. He strongly feels this exercise is therefore worth the time and effort. He has found that after he leads this activity several times in class, students actually choose to do it on their own, which argues for the capability of students in applying this approach individually as required by a writing-from-sources project.

---

1. Look at the title of the book or article. What does the title lead you to think this book is about? How might this satisfy to what you need to know?

2. When was the text written? Does this have any relevance to the text's ability to satisfy your information need?

3. Look at the abstract or summary if you can find one. What does this lead you to think the book is about? How might this satisfy to what you need to know?

4. If the text is a book:

   a. Look at the index. What entries have the most pages? What does this lead you to believe is important to the author? How might this satisfy what you need to know?

   b. Look at the table of contents. What does this lead you to believe is important to the author? How might this satisfy what you need to know?

5. If the text is a scholarly article:

   a. Does it have a literature review? Is this likely to be old information or new?

   b. Did the authors conduct their own study? If so, what were their main results?

6. Is this text worth the time to be more carefully read? If yes, continue. If no, find another text and start these questions again.

7. Now, read the relevant parts of the texts. Use your predictions to help you keep an eye out for the big ideas, and identify how the details relate to the central points.

8. How does this text live up to predictions? What does this tell you about predicting next time?

FIGURE 4.4
Sample activity for predicting

5. Determining Main Ideas

It is my experience in teaching our campus's public speaking class that even intelligent and hard-working students have an extremely difficult time identifying the main ideas of texts and recorded speeches. While the main ideas of the materials we examined together were very obvious to me, the subsequent class discussions revealed that was not the case for the students. Students are likely to need help identifying main ideas in shared texts before they are likely to be able to independently identify the main ideas in the texts they use for writing-from-sources assignments.

In scholarly texts, students can be taught to take advantage of the visual clues and genre conventions that can help readers recognize main ideas. Articles in the sciences and social sciences tend to have predictable anatomies, with distinct sections, often clearly marked with subheadings, for the introduction, literature review, methodology, results, and conclusion. Humanities articles may have less predictable parts, but still often use subheadings that often give clues to the main ideas of each section. Students should be made aware that older knowledge tends to be at the beginning of articles and newer information in the second half, particularly in empirical studies in the sciences and social sciences.[63] This has important implications for how students use and cite information from such texts. Instructing students to read such sections in an order other than they were written may help enable students to identify the main ideas in scholarly articles. Charts and diagrams may also provide students with clues to texts' main ideas. If the author or indexer has written an adequate abstract, then the main ideas should be neatly summarized at the beginning of an article, though students will likely still require practice in demonstrating comprehension through paraphrasing exercises. Within books, there are indexes, tables of contents, subheadings, and graphics that can provide clues that point to authors' main ideas.

However, readers must not only be able to identify what the author thinks are the main ideas, they must also be able to look at a text through the lens of their own rhetorical goal. There may be a detail in a text that becomes the most important idea to be retrieved from that article when it is read in order to write. Novice readers need prompts and questions to help them identify what main ideas or details help them meet their information need. Many of the sample activities in this chapter have incorporated such questions to help students keep an eye on how a given text meets their rhetorical purpose, although graphic organizers or guided practice activities can also be designed specifically to help students keep this in mind (figure 4.5).

As you read this text, think about how it relates to your topic or tentative thesis. In the left column, state or summarize information found in the text. Then decide if it is a main idea or a detail from the author's perspective. (How much time does he or she spend on it?) In the far right column, describe how/if this information meets your information goals.

What am I hoping to find out by reading this text?

What I found:	Main idea or detail?	How does this relate to my rhetorical purpose?

FIGURE 4.5
Sample activity for identifying main ideas

6. Using Fix-Up Options

Moreillon writes, "Monitoring [one's] own meaning making and getting back on the road when [one] has lost [one's] way may be one of the most difficult tasks for any reader."[64] Readers of all levels need to be able to recognize when they do not understand a text and move through the necessary strategies to overcome comprehension barriers, but this is not a naturally acquired skill for most learners. Most novice readers do not have the metacognitive skills to even recognize they have lost comprehension, let alone have a repertoire of strategies to resort to in order to find a solution to the problem.

Once a reader determines he or she has lost comprehension, the most basic problem-solving strategy is to reread the text. If the text contains unfamiliar vocabulary words, the students should underline the unfamiliar words during the rereading. Often, a reader's schema will use the context of an unknown word to figure out the meaning of a sentence. However, if the underlined words seem to be inhibiting comprehension, the next step should be to look up such words in a general or discipline-specific dictionary, then again reread the text. It can also help a reader to "think aloud" through a comprehension problem-solving activity, either verbally or with pencil and paper. Many of the other strategies in this section can be used as fix-up strategies, including activating background knowledge, using sensory images, questioning, predicting, and determining main ideas. If these fail, then sometimes a reader simply needs to read as if he or she understands the meaning.[65] Sometimes copying quotes into notes allows readers to set aside text they feel is important but do not yet understand so that they can come back to it when better informed or when putting together information from multiple sources.

Moreillon says that students should be encouraged to mark up texts to indicate their level of comprehension, either directly in the text or by using sticky notes.[66] They can use numbers from 0 to 3 to indicate their level of comprehension for each paragraph, with 0 meaning they understand nothing and 3 that they understand perfectly (figure 4.6). When they are done with their first reading, they will be able to understand where they achieved comprehension, where they lost it, and where they regained it. They can then annotate what strategies they used to try to regain comprehension in weak paragraphs and how successful they were. Having physical indicators of their thought processes will help them develop awareness of where they are having problems and encourage them to seek their own solutions.

1. Read your text straight through with a pencil in hand. Next to each paragraph, write a number between 0 and 3 to indicate your level of understanding of what that paragraph is trying to say, with 0 meaning you do not understand it at all and 3 meaning you feel very confident that you fully understand the meaning.

2. Go back and reread the article, reading paragraphs that you gave less than a 3 particularly carefully. Would you change your rating of any of these paragraphs after a second, careful time through?

3. For those paragraphs that are still a 0 or 1, what would help you understand them?

   a. Is there a lot of unfamiliar vocabulary? If so, underline the unfamiliar words and look them up in a dictionary or encyclopedia.

   b. Write down what you know about the topic in the paragraph. Does thinking about what you already know help you understand the content better?

   c. What do you know about the genre type? For example, is it a scholarly article? If so, does it follow a science/social sciences format with a literature review, methodology, results, and discussion? If so, can you understand what is most important by rereading the introduction and discussion in the article?

   d. Under what context was this text written? Think about who, what, where, and why the text was written. Does this help you understand the text any better, or does it reveal things you need to find out in order to understand the text?

FIGURE 4.6
Sample activity for using fix-up options

7. Believing/Doubting Game

The concept of the Believing/Doubting Game originally comes from Elbow, although Bean, Chappell, and Gillam develop it more fully.[67] They suggest that readers use low-stakes writing to describe all the reasons why they do believe a text, then separately write all the reasons why they doubt it. They explain, "In the 'believe' portion, you try to look at the world through the text's perspective, adopting its ideology, actively supporting its ideas and values. You search your mind for any life experiences or memories of reading and research that help you sympathize with and support the author's view or ideas."[68] The believing part of this exercise helps readers to read a text sympathetically, something Adler and Van Doren say is critical to understanding and fair evaluation.[69]

For the doubting side of this activity, Bean, Chappell, and Gillam write, "Like an antiballistic missile, the doubting game lets you shoot down ideas that you don't like…. Here you try to think of all of the problems, limitations, or weaknesses in the author's argument. You brainstorm for personal experiences or memories from reading and research that refute or call into question the author's view."[70] Students often feel as if published authors cannot be challenged. This part of the exercise encourages them to not only question the authority of an author, but also to think critically about the necessary boundaries and limitations the author worked within and whether or not they are compatible with readers' own rhetorical goals.

The Believing/Doubting Game strategy makes students aware of how they are drawing on their background knowledge, beliefs, values, and assumptions as they make meaning from and evaluate a source. Such conscious acknowledgment is important not only for evaluation, but also for comprehension. For example, Meier and Richter found that students remembered and processed information differently according to whether the new information was compatible with their previously held beliefs.[71] They found that helping students to be aware of the beliefs and knowledge they brought to the reading transaction helped students more fairly process both belief-consistent and belief-inconsistent texts. While they did not use the Believing/Doubting Game to make students aware of their beliefs, it would be a useful tool in promoting such critical thinking (figure 4.7).

1. Summarize the author's main point:

2. For the next five minutes, freewrite about all of the reasons you can find to agree with his/her argument:

3. For the next five minutes, freewrite about all of the reasons you can find to disagree with his/her argument:

FIGURE 4.7
Sample activity for the Believing/Doubting Game

Conclusion

Research has suggested that the disappointing quality of student research papers is often not primarily a problem of writing ability, but rather one of reading ability.[72] Students have not often been exposed to the scholarly texts required by college writing-from-sources assignments before arriving at college, and these scholarly texts were written for an audience with much higher levels of background knowledge in the discipline. At most institutions, students are generally left to figure out how to read these sources on their own, though many fail to do so. If librarians are interested in helping students to *use* information offered by academic libraries and not just *find* it, reading comprehension is a logical place in which to start.

Whether or not librarians are able to teach reading comprehension directly, they should be aware of how they talk about the sources students are being asked to read because it makes a difference in how students approach writing-from-sources assignments. Holliday and Rogers write, "The ways in which librarians and instructors frame information literacy have significant implications for learning."[73] If educators focus on the type and number of sources, that is what students will focus on when completing their assignments.[74] Likewise, if librarians overemphasize *finding* information and not *using* information, students are more likely to think this is the point of the research paper assignment.[75] If educators emphasize sources as containers, and information as static, that is how students will interpret the task. However, if educators expect students to interpret and use the information, then they must provide students with the instructional support that will enable them to meet expectations.

Notes

1. Louise M. Rosenblatt, *The Reader, the Text, the Poem: The Transactional Theory of the Literary Work* (Carbondale: Southern Illinois University Press, 1978), ix.
2. Barbara Fister, "Teaching the Rhetorical Dimensions of Research," *Research Strategies* 11, no. 4 (1993): 213.
3. Wendy Holliday and Jim Rogers, "Talking about Information Literacy: The Mediating Role of Discourse in a College Writing Classroom," *portal: Libraries and the Academy* 13, no. 3 (2013): 257–71.
4. Sandie Friedman and Robert Miller, "Launching Students toward Source-Based Writing: An Introduction for Librarians," *College and Research Libraries News* 77, no. 4 (2016): 201.
5. April Cunningham and Richard Hannon, "Reinforcing College Reading Strategies in the Library Classroom," *LOEX Quarterly* 40, no. 1 (2013): 7–9.
6. Judi Moreillon, *Coteaching Reading Comprehension Strategies in Secondary School*

Libraries: Maximizing Your Impact (Chicago: American Library Association, 2012), 2.

7. Michelle Holschuh Simmons, "Librarians as Disciplinary Discourse Mediators: Using Genre Theory to Move toward Critical Information Literacy," *portal: Libraries and the Academy* 5, no. 3 (2005): 299.

8. Margy MacMillan and Stephanie Rosenblatt, "They've Found It. Can They Read It? Adding Academic Reading Strategies to Your IL Toolkit," in *Creating Sustainable Community: ACRL 2015, March 25–28, 2015, Portland Oregon: Conference Proceedings*, ed. Dawn M. Mueller, 757, http://www.ala.org/acrl/sites/ala.org.acrl/files/content/conferences/confsandpreconfs/2015/MacMillan_Rosenblatt.pdf.

9. Mortimer Jerome Adler and Charles Van Doren, *How to Read a Book*, rev. and updated ed. (New York: Simon and Schuster, 1972), x.

10. US Department of Education, Institute of Education Sciences, "Are the Nation's Twelfth-Graders Making Progress in Mathematics and Reading?" accessed August 15, 2016, http://www.nationsreportcard.gov/reading_math_g12_2013/#.

11. Ruth Schoenbach, Cynthia Greenleaf, Christine Cziko, and Lori Hurwitz, *Reading for Understanding: A Guide to Improving Reading in Middle and High School Classrooms* (San Francisco: Jossey-Bass, 1999); Simon A. Lei, Kerry A. Bartlett, Suzanne E. Gorney, and Tamra R. Herschbach, "Resistance to Reading Compliance among College Students: Instructors' Perspectives," *College Student Journal* 44, no. 2 (2010): 219–29.

12. Gregg W. Wentzell, Laurie Richlin, and Milton D. Cox, "Exploring Reading and Writing in College: A Message from the Editors," *Journal on Excellence in College Teaching* 22, no. 3 (2011): 1–3.

13. Rebecca Moore Howard, Tricia Serviss, and Tanya K. Rodrigue, "Writing from Sources, Writing from Sentences," *Writing and Pedagogy* 2, no. 2 (2010): 177–92.

14. Wendy Holliday, Betty Dance, Erin Davis, Britt Fagerheim, Anne Hedrich, Kacy Lundstrom, and Pamela Martin, "An Information Literacy Snapshot: Authentic Assessment across the Curriculum," *College and Research Libraries* 76, no. 2 (2015): 178.

15. Moreillon, *Coteaching Reading Comprehension Strategies*; Schoenbach et al., *Reading for Understanding*; Jean-François Rouet, M. Anne Britt, Robert A. Mason, and Charles A. Perfetti, "Using Multiple Sources of Evidence to Reason about History," *Journal of Educational Psychology* 88, no. 3 (1996): 479.

16. Schoenbach et al., *Reading for Understanding*.

17. Maryanne Wolf, *Proust and the Squid: The Story and Science of the Reading Brain* (New York: HarperCollins, 2007), 163.

18. Melissa Bowles-Terry, Erin Davis, and Wendy Holliday, "'Writing Information Literacy' Revisited: Application of Theory to Practice in the Classroom," *Reference and User Services Quarterly* 49, no. 3 (2010): 226.

19. Simmons, "Librarians as Disciplinary Discourse Mediators," 299.

20. Andrea Baer, "Recontextualizing Information, Reembodying Pedagogical Practice" (presentation, Pennsylvania Library Association, College and Research Division Spring Workshop, Scranton, PA, May 20, 2016); James P. Purdy and Joyce R. Walker, "Liminal Spaces and Research Identity: The Construction of Introductory Composition Students as Researchers," *Pedagogy: Critical Approaches to Teaching Literature Language Composition and Culture* 13, no. 1 (2013): 9–41.

21. Rosenblatt, *The Reader, the Text, the Poem*.

22. Ibid., 24.

23. Adler and Van Doren, *How to Read a Book*.

24. Doug Brent, *Reading as Rhetorical Invention: Knowledge, Persuasion, and the Teaching of Research-Based Writing* (Urbana, IL: National Council of Teachers of English, 1992).

25. Ibid.

26. David E. Rumelhart and Andrew Ortony, "The Representation of Knowledge in Memory," in *Schooling and the Acquisition of Knowledge*, ed. Richard C. Anderson, Rand J. Spiro, and William E. Montague (Hillsdale, NJ: Lawrence Erlbaum Associates, 1977), 111.

27. Brent, *Reading as Rhetorical Invention*, 30.

28. Richard C. Anderson, Ralph E. Reynolds, Diane L. Schallert, and Ernest T. Goetz, "Frameworks for Comprehending Discourse," *American Educational Research Journal* 14, no. 4 (1977), 368.

29. Brent, *Reading as Rhetorical Invention*.

30. Rachel Radom and Rachel W. Gammons, "Teaching Information Evaluation with the Five Ws," *Reference and User Services Quarterly* 53, no. 4 (2014): 334–47.

31. Susan R. Goldman, Jason L. G. Braasch, Jennifer Wiley, Arthur C. Graesser, and Kamila Brodowinska, "Comprehending and Learning from Internet Sources: Processing Patterns of Better and Poorer Learners," *Reading Research Quarterly* 47, no. 4 (2012): 356–81.

32. John C. Bean, Virginia A. Chappell, and Alice M. Gillam, *Reading Rhetorically: A Reader for Writers* (New York: Longman, 2002).

33. Adler and Van Doren, *How to Read a Book*, 316.

34. Brent, *Reading as Rhetorical Invention*.

35. Ibid., 61.

36. Johanna Maier and Tobias Richter, "Fostering Multiple Text Comprehension: How Metacognitive Strategies and Motivation Moderate the Text-Belief Consistency Effect," *Metacognition and Learning* 9, no. 1 (2014): 51–74.

37. Brent, *Reading as Rhetorical Invention*.

38. Rouet et al., "Using Multiple Sources of Evidence," 478.

39. Radom and Gammons, "Teaching Information Evaluation with the Five Ws"; Bowles-Terry, Davis, and Holliday, "'Writing Information Literacy' Revisited"; Joel M. Burkholder, "Redefining Sources as Social Acts: Genre Theory in Information Literacy Instruction," *Library Philosophy and Practice 2010* (August 2010): 5, http://unllib.unl.edu/LPP/burkholder.pdf; Kuglitsch, "Teaching for Transfer."

40. Bowles-Terry, Davis, and Holliday, "'Writing Information Literacy' Revisited," 228.

41. Brent, *Reading as Rhetorical Invention*, xv.

42. Burkholder, "Redefining Sources as Social Acts."

43. Ibid.

44. Ibid., 2.

45. Bowles-Terry, Davis, and Holliday, "'Writing Information Literacy' Revisited," 226.

46. Schoenbach et al., *Reading for Understanding*.

47. Moreillon, *Coteaching Reading Comprehension Strategies*, 70.

48. Moreillon, *Coteaching Reading Comprehension Strategies*; Bean, Chappell, and Gillam, *Reading Rhetorically*.

49. Bean, Chappell, and Gillam, *Reading Rhetorically*, 16.

50. Mardy Grothe, *I Never Metaphor I Didn't Like: A Comprehensive Compilation of History's Greatest Analogies, Metaphors, and Similes* (New York: Collins, 2008), 4.

51. Ibid.
52. Genie Z. Laborde, *Influencing with Integrity: Management Skills for Communication and Negotiation* (Palo Alto, CA: Science and Behavior Books, 1983), 27.
53. Moreillon, *Coteaching Reading Comprehension Strategies*.
54. Ellin Oliver Keene and Susan Zimmermann, *Mosaic of Thought: Teaching Comprehension in a Reader's Workshop* (Portsmouth, NH: Heinemann, 1997).
55. Victoria Stein, "Elaboration: Using What You Know," in *Reading-to-Write: Exploring a Cognitive and Social Process* (New York: Oxford University Press, 1990), 145.
56. Moreillon, *Coteaching Reading Comprehension Strategies*.
57. Ibid., 48.
58. Gary R. Hafer, *Embracing Writing: Ways to Teach Reluctant Writers in Any College Course* (San Francisco: Jossey-Bass, 2014).
59. Benedict Carey, *How We Learn: The Surprising Truth about When, Where, and Why It Happens* (New York: Random House, 2014), 102.
60. Laborde, *Influencing with Integrity*.
61. Donna Witek, e-mail message to author, October 6, 2015.
62. Adler and Van Doren, *How to Read a Book*.
63. Cunningham and Hannon, "Reinforcing College Reading Strategies."
64. Moreillon, *Coteaching Reading Comprehension Strategies*, 139.
65. I. A. Richard as cited in Bean, Chappell, and Gillam, *Reading Rhetorically*, 36.
66. Moreillon, *Coteaching Reading Comprehension Strategies*.
67. Peter Elbow, *Everyone Can Write: Essays toward a Hopeful Theory of Writing and Teaching Writing* (New York: Oxford University Press, 2000); Bean, Chappell, and Gillam, *Reading Rhetorically*.
68. Bean, Chappell, and Gillam, *Reading Rhetorically*, 84.
69. Adler and Van Doren, *How to Read a Book*.
70. Bean, Chappell, and Gillam, *Reading Rhetorically*, 84.
71. Maier and Richter, "Fostering Multiple Text Comprehension."
72. Howard, Serviss, and Rodrigue, "Writing from Sources, Writing from Sentences."
73. Holliday and Rogers, "Talking about Information Literacy," 258.
74. Burkholder, "Redefining Sources as Social Acts"; Holliday and Rogers, "Talking about Information Literacy."
75. Fister, "Teaching the Rhetorical Dimensions of Research."

CHAPTER 5

High-Stakes Writing-from-Sources

Instruction on the research process… [typically]… deals with
the beginning and the end of the process (using the library
and writing drafts), but it has a gaping hole in the middle
where much of the real work of knowledge construction is
performed.

—*Brent*[1]

The basic premise of this book is that academic librarians can go beyond
helping students *find* information to helping them *use* information.
Chapter 4 explored how librarians can help students use information
through improving student reading comprehension skills. This chapter will
discuss how librarians can collaborate with teaching faculty to support students' ability to write their own texts based on what they have learned from
the texts of others through assignment design and instructional support. Writing-from-sources assignments that push students past reporting to creating an
original argument have enormous potential for transforming students' knowledge and developing disciplinary expertise. Brent writes, "In all its complexity and messiness, writing from sources can expose students to 'unresolved
dilemmas' and to the difficulties of grappling with them for the benefit of an
audience."[2] Information literacy instruction that promotes this kind of disciplinary learning will undoubtedly be more effective for students and more satisfying for librarians.

Throughout this book, the research *process* is emphasized over the
product as a way of distributing the enormous cognitive demands of writing-from-sources. Focusing on the research process will help educators

assist students in moving from what Bereiter and Scardamalia call "knowledge telling" to "knowledge transforming."[3] Knowledge telling is the kind of writing that comes to everyone naturally and is encouraged in low-stakes writing assignments such as those described in previous chapters. However, knowledge *transforming* is much more rare and difficult to achieve. Bereiter and Scardamalia write, "For those who do use it, the [knowledge transforming] model provides both the promise of higher levels of literacy quality and… the opportunity to gain vastly greater cognitive benefits from the process of writing itself."[4] It is only through the struggle writers undergo as they wrestle with the content space (what to say) and the rhetorical space (how to say it) that their knowledge can be *transformed*. Bereiter and Scardamalia stress that it is only by looking at the writer's *process*, and not only the end *product*, that a reader can tell if knowledge transformation has taken place. Undergraduate students are capable of transforming their knowledge, and librarians can play an important role in helping them achieve this.

Assignment Design

One of the largest challenges of information literacy instruction is teaching to someone else's assignment. It is almost always teaching faculty who create research paper assignments, which are frequently problematic for a number of reasons. Leckie feels that many faculty design their assignments based on faulty understandings of what students should be able to do.[5] Many faculty also emphasize the number and types of sources required in students' bibliographies and the number of pages the paper must be, inadvertently encouraging a checklist mentality among students rather than a desire to learn.[6]

Good high-stakes assignment design, as Hafer indicates, makes "effective writing [and learning] more probable."[7] Furthermore, Bean points out that good assignment design allows educators to make the best use of their own time by building feedback opportunities into the assignment and pointing students in the right direction in the first place to prevent a "barrage" of student questions when they encounter problems that could have been avoided.[8] While librarians rarely design discipline-specific writing-from-sources assignments, they can often influence assignment design. Librarians at Emerson College found that teaching faculty were grateful for librarians' pedagogical expertise given that most of the teaching faculty's professional development resources must be spent on disciplinary research rather than becoming better teachers.[9] To help teaching faculty with information literacy pedagogy, they designed both an intensive three-day, paid workshop for teaching faculty and a "Course Design Spa" in which teaching faculty could sign up for individual consultations with librarians and other academic support specialists on a particular day in August. Both summer initiatives emphasized assignment design that promoted the development of critical information literacy skills.

Effective assignment design for writing-from-sources assignments should promote intrinsic motivation through curiosity. Leist discusses how professional academic scholars use research and writing to satisfy curiosity and solve professional problems; they are driven by something about which they want to know more.[10] Kashdan, Steger, and Breen say that providing just the right quantity of "novelty, complexity, uncertainty, and conflict" can promote curiosity.[11] Low-stakes writing assignments have the potential to increase student curiosity by encouraging deeper reflection and critical thinking about what students want to know on their topic, as was briefly explored in chapter 3.

Gocsik described a creative research assignment in which she worked with the campus archivist to use archival photographs to inspire curiosity.[12] Students were initially given only unlabeled photographs of important historical events on campus, and they were asked to speculate on what they thought was happening. They were then gradually given archival texts to piece together an understanding of the situation. The students became very engaged in the research assignment when time was taken at the beginning to inspire curiosity through suspense. As motivation—preferably intrinsic—is vitally important to learning, developing intense curiosity is an important quality of effective assignment design.

Of course, assignment design must also address the cognitive aspects of writing-from-sources. The literature provides more practical guidance in this area. In two separate series of studies on students' research processes, Nelson and Hayes and Flower and colleagues looked into why students' final research papers so commonly failed to meet educators' expectations.[13] One of the most critical findings in both studies was that students have a wide variety of task interpretations (or task representations) when initially deciding what the assignment is asking them to do. Flower explains that task interpretation is not "a single, simple decision, but an extended interpretive process that weaves itself throughout composing."[14] Because task interpretation and the resulting opening moves carry over throughout the process, it is clearly important to look at how students interpret a writing-from-sources assignment. Nelson and Hayes recommended that educators include the following elements into their assignment design to increase the probability that students would adopt a high-investment approach to writing-from-sources assignments: provide timely feedback, focus on high-level goals, provide an audience other than the teacher, and get students writing early in the research process.[15]

Additionally, a constructivist approach to designing writing-from-sources assignments acknowledges that undergraduates are both novice and expert writers.[16] While they have little experience with scholarly, college-level, or real-world writing, they have a "legacy of literate behavior," which includes everything they have been taught about school writing since kindergarten.[17] This experience has led these students to develop deep-rooted habits and assumptions. Ackerman found that students showed no signs of hesitation in interpreting a new assignment, drawing on these old habits and assumptions, of which they were largely unaware. This task interpretation determines their *opening moves*, how they go about completing the task. If those moves are based on incorrect assumptions that are never checked, the students frequently turn in an uninteresting, poorly revised regurgitation of bits and pieces pulled from their information sources. As experienced school writers, they feel confident that they understand the task at hand. As novices, they do not have the critical evaluation skills to rethink the problem, question their assumptions, abandon work during revision, and start fresh. While students do not arrive to higher education as blank slates, there may a lot of *unlearning* that must be done before students can progress.

Authenticity is an important quality in assignment design that can increase motivation and help direct students' cognitive efforts in the right direction. Assignment design can be made more authentic by addressing issues of audience, purpose, and genre, often called the "Writing Trinity" by compositionists. Writing assignments in which the only audience is the instructor encourage students to view the purpose of the research paper as *testing* rather than *communicating*. Social media tools such as blogs and *Wikipedia* and class presentations of student research have the potential to open up students' work to a broader and more authentic audience. The audience presented in the assignment can also be a fictional one. Kelly asked students to imagine they were interns at the World Bank's Water and Sanitation Division and had been asked to write a project proposal that required research (she provided the sources) to support their argument for why their proposed project deserved to be funded.[18] Students had a clear audience to address: the World Bank committee, which allocates financial resources for special projects. She found that, while students at first struggled to understand the assignment, as they rarely had seen problem-based learning assignments before, most of the groups did very well.

Just as a lack of audience is a problem for students writing the traditional research paper, so is a lack of purpose. Schwegler and Shamoon conducted interviews and found that while teaching faculty create research paper assignments with the idea that students will analyze their resources to construct an argument, students view the assignment as informative and factual, "designed to show off knowledge of library skills and documentation procedures."[19] Hafer writes that assignments must "infuse writing with a purpose, an aim to ground students in writing that accomplishes something outside of itself…. Traditional purposes are to persuade, to evaluate, to show causes or effects, to propose. Have students notice that writing is poised to do something to someone."[20] When professional researchers write, their purpose is not only to inform their audience of what they have discovered through research, but also to persuade them that the discovery is important. In problem-based learning, the purpose is frequently to persuade an imaginary authority to accept a proposed solution to a real-world problem. Based on the evidence in the LIS literature on problem-based learning and my own local observations, students respond well to authentic purposes for research and writing.

Without a clear sense of audience and purpose, a generic research paper assignment will also be unlikely to fit within an existing genre. A genre is a set of conventions of writing that are deeply rooted in a social context. Understanding genres is a key component of tying writing-from-sources assignments to developing disciplinary knowledge. It is working within genres that are authentic to the discipline—both through reading and writing—that students come to understand how people know what they know in the discipline and how they can begin to participate in disciplinary conversations. Therefore, educators should select genres for writing-from-sources assignments with which experts in the field would engage. Audience, purpose, and genre strongly relate to each other and are critical for developing disciplinary procedural knowledge and authentic learning experiences when writing-from-sources.

Good assignment design can set students up for success. Important qualities of assignment design include encouraging a constructivist approach, curiosity, and authenticity. As educators and students struggle to speak the same language—particularly, it seems, in writing-from-sources assignment directions—it will be important to take advantage of the formative assessment potential contained within low-stakes writing assignments early in the research process so that educators can make sure students truly understand what the assignment is asking them to do. Over time, good assignment design and formative assessment activities can help educators and students share an understanding of the educational purpose for writing-from-sources assignments.

Instructional Supports

In conjunction with developing solid and authentic writing-from-sources assignments, librarians and teaching faculty should consider how they can design adequate instructional support for students in the process of research. As was introduced in chapter 2, Vygotsky asserts that students have a level of actual development that represents what they are *independently* capable of achieving, and a potential level of development, which is what they are capable of doing *with the assistance of others*, particularly educators and classmates. In between the actual and potential levels of development is the zone of proximal development at which educators should target their instruction and scaffolding efforts. Scaffolds are the various forms of support that educators provide students that enable the students to surpass their actual level of development. Over time, scaffolds are gradually removed as students become increasingly independent learners.

While these research support activities are traditionally taught, assigned, read, graded, and given feedback on by teaching faculty, students could gain much from librarians' involvement as well. Teaching faculty and librarians bring complementary skill sets and perspectives into the classroom. Teaching faculty are experts in their disciplines, while librarians are experts in research and the library resources. Furthermore, as disciplinary outsiders, librarians are likely to be more aware of the peculiarities of a discipline's scholarly communication than the teaching faculty, who are more likely to take such things for granted.[21] As writing-from-sources problems almost always have numerous possible solutions, a variety of suggestions for troubleshooting in writing-from-sources assignments will undoubtedly be invaluable for undergraduate readers and writers.

This section will discuss how educators can scaffold student learning in four areas during the writing-from-sources process. All of these involve initial instruction followed by time to practice or complete an assignment. The assignments should naturally move students toward the writing-from-sources product. Students should receive timely feedback from teaching faculty and librarians on what they are doing well and in what areas they need to improve, with suggestions for surmounting problems they are struggling with.

1. Mini Assignments

Writers at all levels of expertise need to break large assignments into smaller ones. Because novice writers do not have the necessary skills to do this on their own, they need guidance from educators. Hafer calls these mini assignments *briefs*, as in lawyer's briefs.[22] He says that they are "manageable and scaffold in complexity…. In other words, you start high-stakes assignments with elemental components that move your student writers to more complex components of the assignment later on."[23] Such assignments have the added advantage of discouraging plagiarism as students cannot simply turn in a final paper written by someone else if they must also pass checkpoints along the way.[24]

These mini assignments must be authentic to the writing and inquiry process in order to be useful in furthering student learning. Using backward design, educators should think about what experts do in their writing and inquiry processes and how to get students to gradually take on those habits over the course of an individual assignment or over their undergraduate careers.[25] Well-designed mini assignments will spread out students' cognitive load and provide tangible artifacts on which professors can provide meaningful feedback. The more authentic these mini assignments are, the more useful and productive the feedback on them will be to student learning.

While it is already common for professors to break up writing-from-sources assignments into pieces through such mini assignments as annotated bibliographies, outlines, and drafts, it is unclear if such mini assignments are always productive if they are not grounded in composition and reading comprehension theory. For example, annotated bibliographies generally ask students only to summarize information in articles, which Wiley and Voss found does not lead to a deep understanding of source texts.[26] Annotated bibliographies should ask not only for summaries, but also why students believe the information is appropriate to their information tasks and how they plan to use it in their own compositions.[27] Outlines and theses should be flexible and evolve over the writing process.

Having a librarian involved in designing, providing instruction for, and providing feedback on such mini assignments benefits both students and librarians. Students gain another perspective as they look for ways to improve their learning, and librarians gain a better understanding of where students are struggling. Miller describes a situation in which he helped a student find an information source only to have the student admit she did not know what to do with it.[28] He goes on to ask himself, "How much of my work as a librarian consists in interactions like this one, in which I blithely lead a student into what is, for her, a conceptual cul-de-sac? And how many times am I unaware of the problem, because a student lacks the time and energy… to ask?"[29] Librarian involvement in mini assignments can ensure systematic feedback on student understandings and misunderstandings of key information literacy skills.

2. Information Synthesis

One of the most critical areas for educators, perhaps particularly for librarians, to provide more support for students is in synthesizing information from multiple sources. "Synthesize ideas from multiple sources" is one of the knowledge practices under the *Framework*'s "Research as Inquiry" frame, although it is closely related to other knowledge practices, such as organizing information and seeking multiple perspectives. This is a cognitively demanding task that is in the top levels of both the original Bloom's Taxonomy and the Revised Bloom's Taxonomy.[30] The literature on students' research papers frequently complains that this is one of the areas of research assignments where students fare poorly. Brent writes that his students "approached research as they would gathering shells at the beach, picking up ideas with interesting colors or unusual shapes and putting them in a bucket without regard for overall pattern."[31] Howard, Serviss, and Rodrigue discussed students' patchwork writing.[32] Nelson and Hayes found that if two sources disagree, students who took low-investment approaches simply found a third source to break the tie.[33] In all of these cases, students are simply collecting sources without making much effort to draw connections or develop a single situation model from the sources they have read, which severely limits what they learn from writing-from-sources assignments.

An ability to synthesize information from multiple sources is an extremely important skill for graduates to have in all areas of their future lives. Students need to recognize knowledge is a consensus of knowers as they make sense of potentially conflicting information from multiple sources.[34] Wiley and Voss found that students developed a much stronger understanding of history material when writing from multiple sources rather than a single, textbook-like source.[35] Additionally, they found that students learn the material best when they construct an argument rather than a summary or narrative. Wrestling with information from multiple sources is critical for students to achieve knowledge transformation.

With all of the information available in the scholarly literature on how readers make personal meaning from what they read, there is surprisingly little available to help educators understand how those same readers come to a somewhat unified understanding of a topic based on multiple texts. I will therefore provide a description of some of my own synthesizing strategies or strategies that I have used to teach information synthesis:

- **Notecards (digital or paper):** I was taught by a high school English teacher to record *every* piece of information that seemed important onto an individual notecard, which was a good exercise as a learner, but tedious, and it diverted precious time and energy away from focusing on the big picture of the research project. I find it to be more practical to put *main* ideas onto notecards, then sort (and frequently re-sort) the cards into categories as I work out how to organize all of the ideas I want to include in my writing. It is frequently not until I begin looking for connections between notecards that these categories and a logical progression of ideas emerge. Such a process can help me to create initial outlines. I have used both paper and digital notecards and found that each has its own advantages and disadvantages so that paper notecards are more useful to overcome some writing problems and digital are more appropriate for others.

- **Mind maps:** Mind maps (figure 5.1), which have been introduced in previous chapters, are a low-stakes writing strategy that can serve many purposes. As a researcher with a strong visual learning preference, I have found mind maps to be the single most powerful way of sorting otherwise overwhelming amounts of information. I can start with a chapter or section title in the middle of the page and continue by adding subheadings to represent the big ideas I want to address. I can then fill in each section with brief quotes, paraphrases, and drawings (visual metaphors). I frequently include authors' last names to direct myself back to my notes when I write my drafts.

- **Highlighting notes in different colors:** As I write my notes in our institution's online citation management system, I can manipulate or print out my notes as needed. I frequently print out my notes because I find it difficult to maintain flow in writing when flipping between my draft and my notes on a single computer screen. I keep a collection of highlighters in as many colors as possible. On the first page of my notes, I create a color key. Everything in my printed notes on a given category will be highlighted red, another category in blue, and so forth. When I then go to write a section of my draft, my eyes are drawn to that section's corresponding color, and I can more easily manage my information synthesis, even when managing tens or even hundreds of pages of notes.

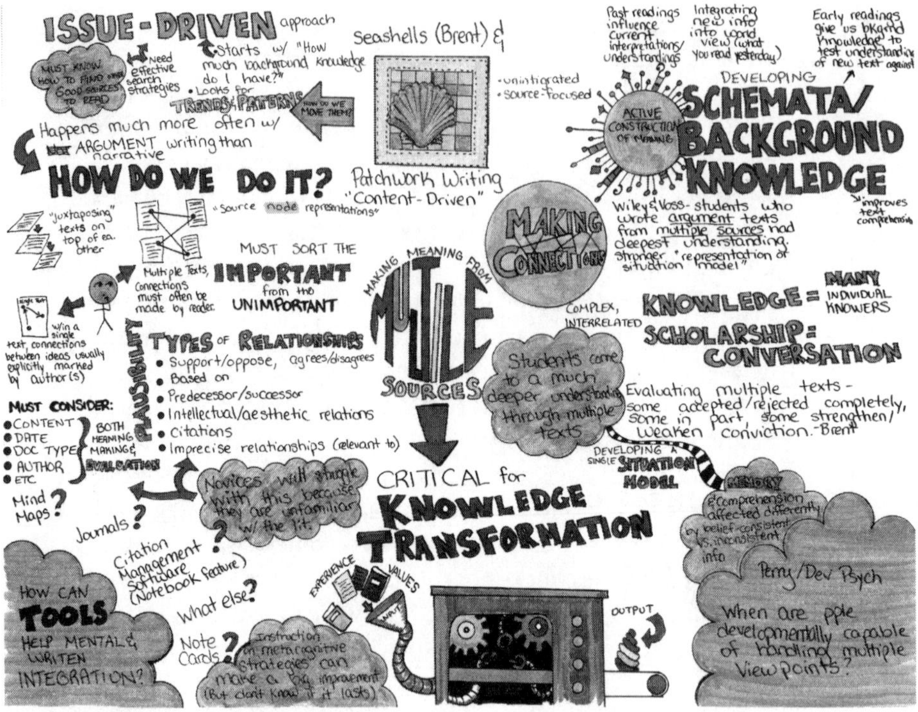

FIGURE 5.1
Mind map created to synthesize information collected on the topic of making meaning from multiple sources

- **Graphic organizers:** Graphic organizers (also known as guided worksheets or guided templates) can be designed by educators to encourage students to read texts rhetorically. They can furthermore set students up for information synthesis between sources. Students can be required to fill out one organizer for each text, and because all of the organizers are identical, they facilitate students' ability to find connections between sources. A single graphic organizer can also be designed to facilitate cross-text connections, such as the organizer (figure 5.2) I designed for a criminal justice class. The professor has found this to positively influence the quality of students' information synthesis.

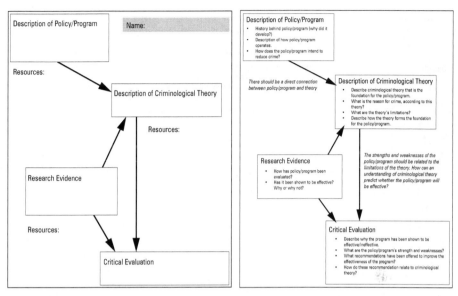

FIGURE 5.2
Graphic organizer to promote information synthesis (directions and template)

These four information synthesis strategies allow students to move pieces of information around in various ways in order to explore their options in developing relationships between ideas until the most useful organization has been identified. There may be additional strategies that educators can use to assist students. I hope that research in this area will improve not only among rhetoric and composition scholars, but also among librarians, and that successful strategies in teaching information synthesis will be shared among educators.

Librarians, as information professionals, should play a key role in helping undergraduates to develop the strategies necessary for dealing with information synthesis and overload. It is unclear how often librarians provide students with in-depth support in this area of the writing-from-sources process. I have identified only two articles in the LIS literature in which librarians teach information synthesis. In the first, Gronemyer and Dollar describe the librarian demonstrating concept mapping to show the multiple ways information can be organized.[36] Because students continued to struggle with information synthesis, in the second year of their collaboration, they spent an entire class on developing this specific skill. The educators provided groups of students with a number of article abstracts and asked each group to identify themes and write a one- or two-paragraph "mini-review" of the abstracts. Each group then shared their review with the class, and they critiqued each other's work. The educators found "the papers written by students that participated in this exercise showed considerably more effective attempts at synthesis than the papers from the year before."[37]

Lundstrom and colleagues also describe a study where the librarian taught a brief lesson on information synthesis, then had students work in small groups where each participant read one article that was unique to themselves and another that was shared between all group members.[38] The students highlighted main points and questions on Post-It notes, which they shared with their group members. As groups, they organized the Post-It notes by theme and individually wrote a paragraph that summarized one of the themes. The educators found that the paragraphs contained higher levels of information synthesis than did the final papers the students wrote several weeks later, although these final papers were better than the control group. They conclude that a high-level skill such as information synthesis needs additional instruction over a longer period of time than the single class in which it was taught in this study.

I have recently begun collaborating with a psychology professor to provide her students with better support in the area of information synthesis. She had been struggling with student literature reviews that were little more than a series of paragraphs that each summarized a source with very little integration. I met with the students during a workshop where I instructed them to label their article printouts with hashtags such as #definitionofconcussion, each hashtag representing an idea they might use in their papers. They were to then transfer each hashtag onto its own notecard to help them focus on looking for similar information in other articles and so they could sort the notecards to help them create outlines for their drafts. Following the project's completion, the instructor reported an improvement of source integration in students' literature reviews. We plan to collaborate over a longer period of time with her future classes to continue the progress made in this experience.

3. Joining the Conversation

In order to avoid student papers that are bland reports of what other people have written on a topic, educators can design and scaffold supports for students so students view their sources and their own writing as part of a conversation within the discipline. This is so central to information literacy that the task force responsible for developing the *Framework* gave this concept its own frame: "Scholarship as Conversation." It is also a common theme in the composition and rhetoric literature. Joining a disciplinary conversation as novices means students will not simply report on what others have said, but will *go beyond those texts* in their own writing to create something new. As few students have received instruction on how to do this, they will need explicit assistance in this area.

Harris provides educators with excellent guidance on how to move students beyond the report paper. He opens his book with, "Whatever else they may do, intellectuals almost always write in response to the work of others…. But to respond is to do more than to recite or ventriloquize; we expect a respondent to add something to what is being talked about."[39] He goes on to describe in detail the ways in which writers respond to texts: coming to terms with, forwarding, countering, and taking an approach. *Coming to terms with* simply means to come to an understanding of the text as an active reader to the point that one can rewrite it and make it one's own. *Forwarding* is a way of building on the ideas of others that one agrees with. *Countering* is a way for a writer to build knowledge by disagreeing with someone else's ideas. *Taking an approach* is "working in the mode of another writer."[40] These four ways of using other people's information can help students move from knowledge telling to knowledge transforming.

A political science professor at my institution has used Harris's *Rewriting* as a required text in an upper-level, writing-intensive course.[41] His goals for using this text were twofold; he wanted to provide students with a foundation of knowledge on which to improve their own writing and to evaluate the scholarship of the texts they would be reading in the class. While the students seemed to be confused about reading about writing, they seemed to better understand how it applied to their own writing after discussing each chapter as a class. The professor said the papers in that class were particularly strong, predominantly in the areas of writing addressed in Harris's book. He reports that he would use the book again, providing additional transparency to students as to why they are reading it.

Another extremely useful resource for educators who want to encourage a more rhetorical use of information sources in student papers is Bizup's article entitled "BEAM: A Rhetorical Vocabulary for Teaching Research-Based Writing."[42] He argues that educators do a disservice to students when they emphasize primary, secondary, and tertiary sources. In doing so, he says that "we attend not to their rhetorical functions or effects but to their relationship to some external point of reference."[43] He contends that "the practice of labeling the first class primary and the second class secondary also subordinates the core intellectual work of writing—the work of interpretation, argumentation, and communication—to the work of research."[44] He says that educators should move the focus from what the sources *are* to what they can *do*. According to Bizup, there are four ways for writers to use sources in their texts:

- **Background:** "materials whose claims a writer accepts as fact, whether these 'facts' are taken as general information or deployed as evidence to support the writer's own assertions."[45]
- **Exhibit:** "materials a writer offers for explication, analysis, or interpretation."[46]
- **Argument:** "materials whose claims a writer affirms, disputes, refines, or extends in some way. To invoke a common metaphor, argument sources are those with which writers enter into a conversation."[47]
- **Method:** "materials from which a writer derives a governing concept or manner of working."[48]

Students can analyze how the texts they read put other texts to use, then follow suit in their own writing.

Due to the emphasis of "Scholarship as Conversation" in the *Framework*, academic librarians are in the process of rethinking students as novice participants in scholarly conversations. The work of Harris and Bizup can assist librarians in this shift of thinking about how they instruct students to use information sources. This does not necessarily require elaborate collaborations with teaching faculty. The intelligible simplicity of Bizup's BEAM provides a means for approaching the narrow confines of the one-shot in a rhetorical fashion. For example, McGinniss works a brief version of Bizup's BEAM into his one-shot library instruction sessions.[49] I have also begun to change how I talk about students' research papers to emphasize participating in a conversation rather than mere reports of others' research.

Some LIS authors have described using BEAM in more course-integrated ways. Rubick collaborated with a composition and rhetoric professor to have students read Bizup's article, discuss the concept of BEAM, and engage in an application exercise where the students labeled four citations in an article as background, exhibit, argument, or method in a think-pair-share exercise.[50] When the students were reluctant to share, the librarian and professor shared theirs, only to find they disagreed with each other. Far from finding this a failure, this led the students to be more willing to discuss their perceptions on how a published author had used sources to participate in the conversation. Students went on to use BEAM in their annotated bibliographies to describe how they planned to use each source in their upcoming essays. The professor found that the resulting final essays were greatly improved over previous semesters.

4. Drafting, Revising, and Rewriting

As this is where students actually *use* information for a purpose, librarians should consider their role in providing troubleshooting support and feedback during students' drafting, revision, and rewriting processes. It is therefore essential that librarians understand the drafting process. While early drafts are a form of low-stakes writing, they deserve to be discussed in this chapter because they lead to mid-stakes second and third drafts and eventually to high-stakes writing in the form of final papers. As described in chapter 3, students should be encouraged to delay judgment in early drafts and focus on getting ideas down on paper. Lamott calls these early pieces of writing "shitty first drafts," though there are many less colorful names such as "discovery drafts" or "zero drafts" that many educators may be more comfortable with.[51] Drafts should be thought of as a workshop or laboratory, where writers test out ideas, relationships between ideas, and words to express thoughts. Failures are inevitable and a necessary part of the knowledge transformation process. It is the critical thinking used in the problem-solving process that is important for student learning.

While early messy drafts are extremely important in the writing-from-sources process, educators eventually need to assist students in revising and rewriting. The main advantage of writing over speech is that it can be revised in order to develop complex ideas. *Revision* means to *re-see* one's work; it *transforms* a piece of writing.[52] Revision is not important only for the improvement of language and grammar, it is also necessary for knowledge transformation to happen. Through multiple rounds of drafts, a writer builds on the complexity of thoughts, ideas, and learning in a piece of writing. True revision requires writers to be willing to throw out pieces of text, which frequently represent significant time and effort, in order to start anew. This is something undergraduate students are extremely reluctant to do.[53]

Developing consistent critical reading skills is likely to help students be able to read their own work critically and look for ways to improve it. Bereiter and Scardamalia point out that "revision requires a language production system capable of operating iteratively, using its own outputs as inputs."[54] Harris develops this idea further by applying his work on coming to terms with, forwarding, countering, and taking an approach to the task of revising one's own work.[55] He translates each of these rhetorical reading strategies to questions writers should ask themselves when revising:

- *What's your project?* What do you want to accomplish in this essay? (Coming to Terms)
- *What works?* How can you build on the strengths of your draft? (Forwarding)
- *What else might be said?* How might you acknowledge other views and possibilities? (Countering)
- *What's next?* What are the implications of what you have to say? (Taking an Approach)[56]

Therefore, assisting students in the critical reading skills presented in chapter 4 helps them to make meaning from others' texts and also to make deeper meaning in their own texts that others can more easily understand.

Hafer distinguishes between revision and rewriting.[57] He defines rewriting as "recast[ing] sentences within paragraphs to discover what options in language are available to the writer, from which the writer can affirm a better version."[58] He says that true revision is nearly impossible to teach and educators should focus instead on rewriting. He supports rewriting throughout the semester in his freshman composition classes by requiring students to get into the habit of finding multiple ways to say the same thing and to justify their choice in which one is the best.

Writers of all ability and experience levels struggle to see what is actually on the page and not what they *meant* to say. Authors in the field of composition share some practical ideas to enable writers to see their own text anew for either revision or rewriting. Hafer suggests printing drafts in new fonts.[59] Elbow suggests reading one's text aloud, which he says "intensifies multiple channels of perception."[60] Scholars too numerous to mention discuss the importance of asking others to read one's work in order to give feedback, whether or not it is required by a professor.

When providing feedback on drafts, educators cannot simply tell students what to do. Students must maintain ownership of their own writing if they are to become more independent writers and learners. Bean says that educators need to treat students' writing as if it were a work in progress and demonstrate the same sensitivity they would show a colleague.[61] Hafer argues that educators should focus their time and energy on commenting on *drafts*, rather than final papers, because this is where instructor feedback fuels student learning.[62] All comments should be given from the perspective of a coach with an eye on helping students improve in quality and independence as writers. Comments on *early* drafts in particular should focus on higher-order concerns such as following the assignment, development of a thesis, quality of argument, and organization.[63] Students can also ask specific questions on where they want help, either verbally in conferences or through short pieces of low-stakes reflective writing.[64] Educators can use students' own questions to guide their focus and feedback as a way to develop the mental habits students need for independent rewriting.

There are numerous articles on collaborations and embedded librarianship experiences in the LIS literature, although none that I have examined go into depth on how the librarian is involved in supporting students' drafting process. I asked three colleagues within the profession if they had ever been involved in providing feedback on drafts in their role as librarians. All had, but not systematically. One had provided feedback on citations only, but did not find this to be valuable. The other two had provided feedback on drafts beyond their official roles as librarians, although one was quick to point out that the work she had done with one student in particular was not scalable to an entire class. I have also recently experienced some informal opportunities to assist students with paper drafts through reference transactions and believe the experience was greatly beneficial to both the students and myself. If librarians provide feedback on drafts, they should not be concerned with grammar; rather they should focus on students' integration of sources, idea organization, logic, and quality of argument as these are the aspects of drafts most relevant to information literacy. However, drafts are particularly time-consuming to read, and time constraints will almost always be an issue for librarians except in the most generous of embedded librarianship situations.

Conclusion

In the previous chapter, I argued that teaching reading comprehension skills was one important way that librarians could move beyond helping students find information to helping them use information. The next step is helping students to synthesize information from multiple sources and present their new worldview on a topic in writing. In this chapter, I have presented information on how assignment design and instructional supports can enhance the likelihood of student success in writing-from-sources assignments. At a minimum, librarians should be aware of what has been presented here so they do not misrepresent the process when they choose how they will speak about the assignment. But librarians and learners could benefit from an increased librarian involvement in students' writing-from-sources processes.

Swanson writes, "The recognition of the need to make good judgments is at the heart of information literacy."[65] Writing and information literacy are each a series of judgments and decisions. Low-stakes and mid-stakes writing can help librarians better understand student decision making. Librarians need to understand and influence student decisions if they are to teach information literacy. Any effort to separate information literacy from reading and writing will be artificial, and therefore detrimental to student learning.

Notes

1. Doug Brent, *Reading as Rhetorical Invention: Knowledge, Persuasion, and the Teaching of Research-Based Writing* (Urbana, IL: National Council of Teachers of English, 1992), 105.
2. Douglass Brent, "The Research Paper and Why We Should Still Care," *Writing Program Administration* 37, no. 1 (2013): 40.
3. Carl Bereiter and Marlene Scardamalia, *The Psychology of Written Composition* (Hillsdale, NJ: L. Erlbaum Associates, 1987).
4. Ibid., 5.
5. Gloria J. Leckie, "Desperately Seeking Citations: Uncovering Faculty Assumptions about the Undergraduate Research Process," *Journal of Academic Librarianship* 22, no. 3 (1996): 201–8.
6. Stephanie Margolin and Wendy Hayden, "Beyond Mechanics: Reframing the Pedagogy and Development of Information Literacy Teaching Tools," *Journal of Academic Librarianship* 41, no. 5 (2015): 602–12.
7. Gary R. Hafer, *Embracing Writing: Ways to Teach Reluctant Writers in Any College Course* (San Francisco: Jossey-Bass, 2014), 81.
8. John C. Bean, *Engaging Ideas: The Professor's Guide to Integrating Writing, Critical Thinking, and Active Learning in the Classroom* (San Francisco: Jossey-Bass, 1996).
9. Anne Barnhart, Ru Story-Huffman, Karla Fribley, Joy Muller, Brenna Helmstutler, and Yan He, "Faculty Are Lifelong Learners So Why Not Teach Them? Information Literacy Instruction Offered to Faculty" (presentation, Association of College and Research Libraries Conference, Portland, OR, March 28, 2015).
10. Susan M. Leist, *Writing to Teach; Writing to Learn in Higher Education* (Lanham, MD: University Press of America, 2006).
11. Todd B. Kashdan, Michael F. Steger, and William E. Breen, "Curiosity," in *Encyclopedia of Social Psychology*, ed. Roy F. Baumeister and Kathleen D. Vohs, vol. 1 (Los Angeles: Sage Publications, 2007), 214.
12. Karen Gocsik, "Reading and Writing Visual Arguments" (presentation, Bucknell University Writing Program Workshop, Lewisburg, PA, January 15, 2016).
13. Jennie Nelson and John R. Hayes, *How the Writing Context Shapes College Students' Strategies for Writing from Sources* (Berkeley, CA: Center for the Study of Writing, Carnegie Mellon University, 1988); Linda Flower, Victoria Stein, John Ackerman, Margaret J. Kantz, Kathleen McCormick, and Wayne C. Peck, *Reading-to-Write: Exploring a Cognitive and Social Process* (New York: Oxford University Press, 1990).

14. Linda Flower, "The Role of Task Representation in Reading-to-Write," in *Reading-to-Write: Exploring a Cognitive and Social Process* (New York: Oxford University Press, 1990), 35.
15. Nelson and Hayes, *How the Writing Context*.
16. John Ackerman, "Translating Context into Action," in *Reading-to-Write: Exploring a Cognitive and Social Process* (New York: Oxford University Press, 1990), 173–93.
17. Ibid., 177.
18. Savannah L. Kelly, "Librarians, Renounce the Research Paper! Using Rhetoric to Improve Assignment Design," *College and Undergraduate Libraries* 21, no. 1 (2014): 90–98.
19. Robert A. Schwegler and Linda K. Shamoon, "The Aims and Process of the Research Paper," *College English* 44, no. 8 (1982): 819.
20. Hafer, *Embracing Writing*, 34.
21. Margy MacMillan and Stephanie Rosenblatt, "They've Found It. Can They Read It? Adding Academic Reading Strategies to Your IL Toolkit," in *Creating Sustainable Community: ACRL 2015, March 25–28, 2015, Portland Oregon: Conference Proceedings*, ed. Dawn M. Mueller, 757–62, http://www.ala.org/acrl/sites/ala.org.acrl/files/content/conferences/confsandpreconfs/2015/MacMillan_Rosenblatt.pdf; Michelle Holschuh Simmons, "Librarians as Disciplinary Discourse Mediators: Using Genre Theory to Move toward Critical Information Literacy," *portal: Libraries and the Academy* 5, no. 3 (2005): 297–311.
22. Hafer, *Embracing Writing*, 84.
23. Ibid.
24. Janet McNeil Hurlbert, Cathleen R. Savidge, and Georgia R. Laudenslager, "Process-Based Assignments: How Promoting Information Literacy Prevents Plagiarism," *College and Undergraduate Libraries* 10, no. 1 (2003): 39–51.
25. Grant P. Wiggins and Jay McTighe, *Understanding by Design* (Alexandria, VA: Association for Supervision and Curriculum Development, 2005).
26. Jennifer Wiley and James F. Voss, "Constructing Arguments from Multiple Sources: Tasks That Promote Understanding and Not Just Memory for Text," *Journal of Educational Psychology* 91, no. 2 (1999): 301–11.
27. John C. Bean in discussion with the author, August 2015.
28. Sandie Friedman and Robert Miller, "Launching Students toward Source-Based Writing: An Introduction for Librarians," *College and Research Libraries News* 77, no. 4 (2016): 198–201.
29. Ibid., 199.
30. Kacy Lundstrom, Anne R. Diekema, Heather Leary, Sheri Haderlie, and Wendy Holliday, "Teaching and Learning Information Synthesis," *Communications in Information Literacy* 9, no. 1 (2015): 60–82.
31. Brent, *Reading as Rhetorical Invention*, xiii.
32. Rebecca Moore Howard, Tricia Serviss, and Tanya K. Rodrigue, "Writing from Sources, Writing from Sentences," *Writing and Pedagogy* 2, no. 2 (2010): 177–92.
33. Nelson and Hayes, *How the Writing Context*.
34. Brent, *Reading as Rhetorical Invention*.
35. Wiley and Voss, "Constructing Arguments from Multiple Sources."
36. Kate Gronemyer and Natalie Dollar, "Collaboration in Speech Communication: A Case Study in Faculty-Librarian Collaboration to Teach Undergraduates to Write a

Literature Review," in *Embedded Librarians: Moving beyond One-Shot Instruction*, ed. Cassandra Kvenild and Kaijsa Calkins (Chicago: Association of College and Research Libraries, 2011), 107–19.

37. Ibid., 113.
38. Lundstrom et al., "Teaching and Learning Information Synthesis."
39. Joseph Harris, *Rewriting: How to Do Things with Texts* (Logan, UT: Utah State University Press, 2006), 1–2.
40. Ibid., 74.
41. Daniel C. Tagliarina, e-mail message to author, October 30, 2015.
42. Joseph Bizup, "BEAM: A Rhetorical Vocabulary for Teaching Research-Based Writing," *Rhetoric Review* 27, no. 1 (2008): 72–86.
43. Ibid., 73.
44. Ibid., 74–75.
45. Ibid., 75.
46. Ibid.
47. Ibid., 75–76.
48. Ibid., 76.
49. Jeremy McGinniss in discussion with the author, August 2015.
50. Kate Rubick, "Flashlight: Using Bizup's BEAM to Illuminate the Rhetoric of Research," *Reference Services Review* 43, no. 1 (2015): 98–111.
51. Anne Lamott, "Shitty First Drafts," in *Language Awareness: Readings for College Writers*, ed. Paul A. Eschholz, Alfred F. Rosa, and Virginia P. Clark, 9th ed. (Boston: Bedford/St. Martin's, 2005), 93–96; Donald Morison Murray, *A Writer Teaches Writing: A Practical Method of Teaching Composition*, 2nd ed. (Boston: Houghton Mifflin, 1985); Alan Ziegler, *The Writing Workshop Note Book: Notes on Creating and Workshopping* (New York: Soft Skull Press, 2007).
52. Hafer, *Embracing Writing*.
53. Ackerman, "Translating Context into Action."
54. Bereiter and Scardamalia, *The Psychology of Written Composition*, 83.
55. Harris, *Rewriting*.
56. Ibid., 99.
57. Hafer, *Embracing Writing*.
58. Ibid., 106.
59. Ibid.
60. Peter Elbow, *Vernacular Eloquence: What Speech Can Bring to Writing* (Oxford: Oxford University Press, 2012), 237.
61. Bean, *Engaging Ideas*.
62. Hafer, *Embracing Writing*.
63. Bean, *Engaging Ideas*.
64. Hafer, *Embracing Writing*.
65. Troy Swanson, "Information Literacy, Personal Epistemology, and Knowledge Construction," *College and Undergraduate Libraries* 13, no. 3 (2006): 101.

CHAPTER 6

Turning Theory into Practice

> The writing process and the research process are so inti-
> mately intertwined in the academic work of students that any
> effort to separate the two compromises the effort to create an
> accurate model for working with students.
>
> —Elmborg[1]

This book has focused heavily on the theories drawn from many disciplines related to learning through writing-from-sources assignments.
Educational theories are extremely important because they give educators an idea of where they want to go and a framework for getting there.
However, such theories are important only if they improve teaching practice
and student learning. As Elmborg writes, "'Theory' can be valued, but only
if it accurately correlates with what happens in the day-to-day activities of
the work to be done."[2] This book has left a few loose ends that need to be addressed regarding the transition between theory and practice while moving
toward a more rhetorical, process-based approach to information literacy
instruction. The most obvious of these loose ends is a need for practical suggestions for making the time to teach information literacy as suggested in
this book. But just as important are other concerns about the significance
of reflective teaching and managing change. This chapter will address these
concerns in a question-and-answer format in order to begin answering the
overarching question of "What next?"

Question 1:
Is There a Recommended Framework for Implementation That Would Help Librarians Put This Theory into Practice?

Brookfield's book *Becoming a Critically Reflective Teacher* can be a powerful framework for moving forward with a dramatically different approach to information literacy instruction.[3] Reflection on one's teaching helps educators consciously examine what works well and what needs to be changed in their classrooms. It can be applied not only to one's previous instruction, but also to current instructional experiments, such as a move to process-based information literacy. Brookfield says that there are four complementary lenses that educators can use to become more holistically reflective in their teaching: one's autobiography, feedback from students, theory, and colleagues. The previous five chapters of this book have presented a great deal of theory from the fields of rhetoric and composition, psychology, and education and included suggestions on using process-based information literacy to conduct formative assessment. This chapter will encourage individual librarians to make this transition in a community of librarian colleagues and teaching faculty collaborators. What has not yet been addressed is the first lens, that of one's autobiography.

Brookfield claims that some of the most powerful influences that shape educators' teaching are their own memories of teachers they admired and their own experiences as learners. However, reflective practice goes beyond looking at one's *past* as a learner; it also requires present experience on which to reflect. Brookfield goes on to say, "Of all the methods available for changing how we teach, putting ourselves regularly in the role of learner has the greatest long-term effects."[4] This means that librarians (and teaching faculty) need to seek out opportunities to write from sources, reflect on those experiences, and tie those reflections to their assignment design and instructional support of students' writing-from-sources. Just as composition scholars such as Hafer and Elbow assert that writing teachers need to write, and reading apprenticeship theories require educators to reflect on their own reading, librarians need to continue to practice the information literacy skills they teach.[5]

While librarians do a lot of writing in their everyday jobs, such as reports, e-mails, marketing materials, website copy, and newsletters, the LIS literature indicates that few academic librarians write for publication.[6] It is therefore unlikely that many continue to practice anything that resembles the writing-from-sources they teach students to engage in. Writing for publication is one way that librarians can gain more recent experience with writing-from-sources and knowledge creation. However, there are several additional ways that librarians can obtain recent experience with writing-from-sources. One alternative is for librarians to periodically take a class (either a stand-alone class or one that is part of an additional degree or certification) that includes writing-from-sources assignments. Another is to complete some of the research assignments in courses for which they teach information literacy sessions. Ongoing reflections on one's own writing-from-sources experience combined with composition and rhetoric theory, student assessment data, and feedback from colleagues create a well-rounded framework for improving one's support for process-based information literacy instruction.

Question 2:
What Do Librarians Need to Give Up in Order to Move toward a Rhetorical, Process-Based Approach to Information Literacy Instruction?

It will require time and energy for librarians to learn about and move toward a process-based and rhetorical concept of information literacy. Most of such resources are already allocated elsewhere in academic libraries. No matter how effective librarians' efforts are in improving student learning, institutions of higher education are highly unlikely to greatly increase library staff size to accommodate the increased workload. Many readers are likely to have read the first five chapters of this book wondering how this kind of support and instruction is possible given librarians' already overloaded schedules and small numbers in comparison to teaching faculty, who also have overloaded schedules.

The good news is that moving toward process-based information literacy instruction is scalable. Individual librarians can work small changes into one-shot information literacy sessions with little collaboration with course instructors. In a one-shot session, McGinniss teaches an abbreviated version of Bizup's BEAM, a method of teaching students to use their information sources that was described in chapter 5.[7] Witek uses reflections on her own professional research and writing processes to construct more authentic answers to students' questions about the research process in one-shot sessions.[8] I have begun to stress to students that the reason professors require scholarly articles is not only because these articles are often more reliable than many web resources, but above all because they are a critical part of the process of learning to think and behave like someone in that discipline. Librarians can change how they talk about research with little adjustment in the time they spend on instruction.

However, a more effective approach to teaching process-based information literacy is not compatible with a purely one-shot approach to instruction. Just as students' inquiry and writing processes need to be spread out, librarians should be able to integrate their instruction and support throughout that process, which takes time. The term *opportunity cost* describes what one must give up in order to do or have something else.[9] As librarians already have full schedules, spending more time on process-based information literacy instruction will require *not* doing something else. Instruction librarians and administrators will need to value process-based information literacy enough to make time in their schedules to learn about and implement its instruction.

Evangeliste and Furlong coedited a book entitled *Letting Go of Legacy Services* in which various types of librarians describe using "planned abandonment" in order to reallocate resources for innovation.[10] In their introduction, Evangeliste and Furlong write, "Library workers often propose and add new services, but don't always critically examine existing realities in light of our missions, and rarely let go of obsolete or less useful programs. It's terribly difficult, if not impossible, to innovate in big or important ways if you also have to keep doing everything you've always done."[11] They say that planned abandonment is "grounded in assessment-based decision making"[12] where organizations use assessment to critically examine how goals, outcomes, and resources relate to each other. Librarians should be conducting a suite of assessments, not only of public services and collections data, but also of administrative functions in order to determine that their finite resources are being put to the best use. One possible assessment is an analysis of how library staff spend their time in relation to the library's overall mission. At an ACRL 2015 Conference presentation on assessing academic libraries' value, Mengel stated that one of her mottos was "Think bigger, think fewer, think longer term."[13] An analysis of a library's inputs and outputs is likely to reveal areas in which resources, such as librarians' time, can be reallocated to invest in higher-impact practices. Creative thinking, dedication, and partnerships founded on shared teaching goals can help librarians lead the way in making writing-from-sources assignments more significant learning experiences.

Question 3:
Are There Any Time-Management Strategies to Facilitate Process-Based Information Literacy Instruction?

There is an ongoing conversation in the profession about who owns information literacy. Pawley writes, "Ownership of so politically charged a term assigns rights and privileges," which librarians have used to justify staff and other resources.[14] Cowan writes, "Information literacy is still written about, presented, and practiced within libraries and higher education institutions as if it still naturally falls within the purview of libraries and as if librarians are still, somehow, best positioned to create and implement it."[15] Farkas argues that because teaching faculty have so much more time with students, they should assume responsibility for carrying information literacy beyond one-shot sessions.[16] These and other librarians are beginning to realize that it is unrealistic and unhelpful to insist that responsibility for information literacy instruction belongs solely to librarians. Literacy is central to independent learning, and therefore the responsibility for teaching it belongs to everyone in higher education, an attitude that Writing across the Curriculum proponents adopted several decades ago with a fair amount of success.

There are at least four instructional strategies to achieve big changes in information literacy instruction without increasing staff size or overall librarian workload. Some sustainable alternatives to requesting more face-to-face time with students include librarians training teaching faculty, creating tutorials for flipped learning, engaging in various forms of embedded librarianship, and spreading increasingly complex information literacy skills throughout the curricula of individual majors. All of these (including tutorials) require deep levels of collaboration with and trust in the teaching faculty who would share responsibility for teaching information literacy with librarians. The remainder of this section will address each of these strategies in detail.

1. Training the Trainer

Throughout this book, the importance of literacy skills for college graduates has been emphasized. Yet what has also been emphasized is how enormous the task of teaching these skills is. Such skills cannot be adequately taught in information literacy one-shot sessions, just as they cannot be taught in freshman composition alone. Process-based information literacy instruction must start with process-based assignments, and teaching this concept of information literacy takes time. Assignment and curriculum design is clearly within the realm of teaching faculty. Furthermore, teaching faculty have extended time with students to more effectively teach information literacy skills gradually and provide extended practice and meaningful feedback.

However, librarians clearly have their own expertise that is complementary to teaching faculty and therefore have an important role to play in information literacy instruction that does not have to be limited to the one-shot, guest-lecture model. Local programs that support teaching effectiveness as it relates to enhancing information literacy instruction can fill a need among teaching faculty for professional development. Librarians can collaborate with and educate faculty on practices that will improve student learning of information literacy skills. There is growing conversation in the LIS literature and at professional conferences that librarians need to "train the trainer." In this model of information literacy instruction, librarians use their expertise in information literacy and its related pedagogies to act as consultants with teaching faculty rather than strictly as direct educators themselves.

Donovan presented a keynote speech at the Innovative Library Classroom Conference in 2015 where she talked about Indiana University's information literacy instruction program moving from direct instruction to consulting with teaching faculty. Under this program, it is now the teaching faculty, with a librarian's guiding expertise, who embed information literacy into courses over time.[17] Instruction librarians at Indiana were struggling to scale an information literacy program based on the one-shot instruction model due to a number of changes including national and local trends in information literacy instruction, a renovation of the physical space, and staffing. They decided to think beyond what they had traditionally been doing and consider more creative models, such as consulting with teaching faculty. In one of her slides (table 6.1), she compares the qualities of a librarian as instructor versus a librarian as a consultant.

As consultants, librarians ask professors questions such as "What would you need in order to fulfill your information literacy instructional dreams?" They then work to support the faculty and therefore are "indirectly influencing student learning." While the program is still new, they feel that they are having a much bigger impact on student learning of information literacy skills as consultants than they did as direct educators.

TABLE 6.1

Librarian as instructor versus librarian as consultant
(Source: Carrie Donovan, "Shaking Up the Sediment: Re-energizing Pedagogical Practice While Avoiding Bottle Shock" [slides from keynote speech at The Innovative Library Classroom 2015, Radford, VA, May 12, 2015], slide 17, http://www.slideshare.net/TheILC/shake-up-the-sediment.)

Instructor	Consultant
• Direct student contact	• Instructional design
• Everyday interactions with learners	• Librarians' expertise
• Limited involvement	• Influence assignment design
• In the classroom	• Engagement in course design
• Library service provider	• Partner with faculty

In an ACRL 2015 Conference presentation entitled "Leaving the One Shot Behind," Dolinger and Farkas also discussed the concept of training teaching faculty.[18] They said that librarians asked their faculty what skills students needed to succeed on research papers and which ones they (the faculty) taught. The librarians then developed suites of supporting materials, such as online tutorials and printable worksheets, for the teaching faculty to select from in order to fill in the gaps. Dolinger and Farkas stressed that building relationships with faculty is a central element to the success of sustainably moving away from the one-shot model of information literacy instruction and that in developing such relationships, librarians should focus on the educational goals that librarians and teaching faculty share.

As these examples show, the concept of training the trainer can be manifested in many ways. In some cases, it will enhance traditional information literacy one-shot sessions by encouraging teaching faculty to incorporate process-based information literacy into the assignment design and the supporting instruction. In other examples, librarians have very little direct contact with students, just as with many other teaching support professionals on campus, such as those in the writing center. In all of these cases, librarians must build strong relationships with teaching faculty based on mutual trust and respect as they work toward joint educational goals.

2. Tutorials

Clark and Mayer found "overwhelming evidence" that online learning can be as effective as face-to-face learning.[19] Kaplowitz says that online information literacy instruction may allow librarians to be even more student-centered than face-to-face instruction because tutorials can be more adaptable to individual learners' differences, including learning preferences, pace, skill level, schedule, and a need for review.[20] Additionally, online tutorials can include more interactivity, getting *all* users to be active participants in learning. Online tutorials can solve a number of common instruction problems, such as reaching students who are not physically on campus, providing point-of-need assistance when students are conducting their research, and providing information literacy instruction when the need for such instruction is more than library staff can manage. While all of these are important aspects of teaching information literacy through online tutorials, it is the issue of staff time that is most relevant to the content of this chapter.

Online tutorials for information literacy are frequently discussed in the LIS literature. Muir and Heller-Ross briefly describe replacing in-person instruction with tutorials in lower-level classes in order to free time to embed librarians in upper-level classes, which they found effective.[21] Stiwinter describes an initiative to address the fact that her community college did not have enough librarians to reach all English 101 students.[22] They worked with instructors to require that all English 101 students complete a library tutorial. While she admits there were some aspects of the tutorial that needed small improvements, all of their assessments indicated that students were learning from it. In these two examples, librarians invested time up front to create an asynchronous learning object that students could complete at their convenience, freeing librarians to invest their time elsewhere.

Bowles-Terry, Hensley, and Hinchliffe feel that recorded tutorials are particularly good for doing the "grunt work" of basic information literacy instruction and that more complex, conceptual, and advanced skills are better saved for synchronous (whether in-person or online) instruction.[23] Potential topics for tutorials that promote process-based information literacy include individual reading strategies, how to take effective notes from readings, and how to use outlines throughout the writing-from-sources process, to name just a few. Librarians can consider partnering with composition professors or writing center professionals for topics that are not traditionally considered the domain of the library or are outside of the librarians' expertise. Such tutorials could promote foundational knowledge and begin modeling desired behaviors to students, after which educators could offer deliberate opportunities to put such foundational knowledge to practical use with in-class or homework exercises.

While library tutorials are generally aimed at students, libraries may also want to create one or more tutorials aimed at faculty, particularly at large institutions. Such tutorials can be on subjects such as process-based assignments or an introduction to process-based information literacy. They can be posted on library websites or institutional webpages aimed at teaching faculty, shown in departmental or faculty meetings, or linked to in e-mails. Such learning objects for teaching faculty can complement in-person faculty outreach and advocacy.

Appelt and Pendell cite a number of studies that have reported that students do not use online library tutorials unless they are required for class.[24] Our library's website analytics show this to be true at my own institution. Therefore, librarians should partner with teaching faculty to design tutorials that can be integrated into their course content. This partnership would develop tutorials that are more aligned with course content and therefore be more useful to students. As faculty buy-in for tutorials is so important, Appelt and Pendell sought faculty feedback on their library tutorials. Faculty in different disciplines had different needs regarding information literacy tutorials, which demonstrates the importance of collaborating with faculty as early in the tutorial design process as possible so the information literacy tutorials align with teaching faculty's educational goals and assignments.

Before embarking on tutorial creation, it is important to spend some time learning about the qualities of effective online tutorials. One excellent resource for developing a solid understanding of best practices for online tutorials is Clark and Mayer's *E-Learning and the Science of Instruction*, which looks at the cognitive science of online learning.[25] Additionally, the LIS literature provides numerous case studies that allow librarians to learn from others' experience in creating information literacy tutorials. In addition to collaborating with teaching faculty to build tutorials that can be embedded in courses, librarians should keep the following advice in mind:

- Do not underestimate how long good tutorials take to create.
- Keep each tutorial short.
- Balance images and audio.
- Accommodate students with disabilities.
- Keep tutorials up to date (or avoid content that will need frequent updating).

As with all learning, tutorials should include assessment. Formative assessments offer corrective feedback when students provide evidence that they are not meeting the learning targets and encouragement when they are. Such assessments are inherently tied to meaningful interactivity, an important element in designing effective library tutorials.[26] Summative assessments, such as pre- and posttests, can test both student learning and the tutorial as a learning object. Armstrong and Georgas conducted pre- and posttests on their interactive tutorial and found statistically significant gains in student knowledge.[27] They also surveyed students and found that 80 percent of students would recommend the tutorial and 83.3 percent wanted more tutorials like it. Analyzing usage data from tools such as Google Analytics can provide an additional facet to the assessment of tutorials, such as how much use the tutorials receive, on what kind of devices, and how long users are spending on the page. Together, these assessments improve student learning both in the immediate sense (formative assessments) and over time as online learning objects are improved (summative assessments).

3. Sustainable Embedded Librarianship

Embedded librarianship is hard to define because it can represent a wide variety of teaching arrangements. In higher education, it tends to be used to refer to information literacy instruction that is more integrated into the broader course and breaks down the physical, temporal, and affective barriers between librarians and students. Embedded librarianship is more than just spending more time with students; it is about bringing the library to where the students are.[28] While embedded librarianship can use technology to bring the *library* to students without necessarily embedding a *librarian* (i.e., widgets that embed course-specific library resources in learning management systems), embedded librarianship usually means an increased presence of a librarian.[29] Librarians may meet with a class multiple times over a semester or even coteach a class, or they may participate in the course's pages in learning management systems. Farkas emphasizes that it is not critical for the librarian to be available at all times, but it is important to be there at the *right* times.[30]

As with the other strategies described in this chapter, relationships are at the heart of most embedded librarianship initiatives. Librarians become immersed in a course's culture and space.[31] In this model of information literacy instruction, the librarian becomes an integral part of the course curriculum and is tied to what students are doing in a pedagogically logical way.[32] The embedded librarian has opportunities to learn more deeply about and respond to the information literacy needs of students in their courses over time. This changes the relationship that librarians have with students in that they become team members rather than service providers.[33] Booth and colleagues conducted a study of student papers and found that higher levels of librarian involvement with the class for instruction and assignment design led to increasingly greater learning and performance in three areas: attribution, evaluation, and communication.[34] Clearly librarians can play an important role in increasing students' learning outcomes in writing-from-sources assignments.

Isbell and Broaddus describe a course in which the librarian and teaching faculty equally cotaught in order to teach research and writing as "inseparable."[35] Throughout their article, it is clear that the librarian and teaching faculty deeply shared the same educational goals and vision of student success. They were pleased with the experience and student results, but the amount of time required to coteach an entire course was sometimes problematic for the librarian. Witek discusses another instruction collaboration with a composition professor for a class called Rhetoric and Social Media in which she helped design the course, teach, and assess student work, attending the class as often as her other duties would allow.[36] This initial teaching collaboration turned into a long-term teaching and research partnership. The students in each of these case studies showed noteworthy learning improvements due to the significant investment of time and energy on the part of the librarian throughout the duration of the course. The LIS literature contains many additional stories of success with similar examples of time-intensive embedded librarianship.

While embedded librarianship is often time-consuming, librarians have been finding ways to make a bigger impact on student learning by shifting their workload priorities. Some institutions are finding other ways to cover reference desk shifts to allow librarians to spend more time on embedded instruction. Others are focusing embedded efforts on strategically selected classes while cutting down on instruction in other classes. Farkas tackled the problem of making embedded librarianship sustainable in a TechSource workshop where she stressed that librarians should look beyond simply doing *more* teaching, as they do not have time.[37] Rather, librarians should carefully consider the full range of time-intensive, high-touch, and lower-touch approaches. A high-touch approach may involve investing in a strategically selected class or a one-time intensive project that will establish a more manageable long-term arrangement. Lower-touch approaches include using RSS technologies to push alerts when the librarian's attention is needed in online forums. While embedded librarianship has potential for improving relationships with faculty and students as well as greatly improving students' learning outcomes in regard to information literacy, librarians should carefully consider both the long-term and short-term implications of embarking on new embedded librarianship initiatives.

4. Thinking Even Bigger

Academic librarians are increasingly looking at information literacy as it fits into the broader institutional curriculum as a whole. Curriculum mapping and integrating information literacy instruction into departmental and institutional learning goals have many advantages over disjointed one-shot instruction sessions or individual librarians' instructional efforts. It has the potential to increase student learning without additional burdens on librarians' workloads because it shares responsibility for teaching information literacy with teaching faculty and librarians *systematically* spread out increasingly higher-order information literacy skills they want students to learn over students' college careers. It can also help library instruction programs ensure that staffing and instructional resources are properly distributed based on content areas' needs, increase conversations with teaching faculty, and help librarians develop a deeper understanding of the institutional curriculum.[38]

Like embedded librarianship, curriculum mapping can be implemented in many different ways, including at the departmental or institutional level, or even entirely within the library. Arensdorf, Pettitt, and VanLaningham worked with the English department at Loras College to spread information literacy across the English literature major.[39] They were able to get information literacy into the learning outcomes of three strategically chosen courses ending with the departmental capstone. Librarians invested a great deal of time and energy in these three courses in order to teach increasingly complex information literacy skills and topics such as citations, mapping scholarly conversations, and special collections. Curriculum mapping may also occur at the institutional level. Moser and colleagues describe the development of a curriculum mapping initiative at Oxford College, a two-year liberal arts institution.[40] After the results of NITLE's Research Practices Survey revealed a number of faulty assumptions on the part of teaching faculty, students, and librarians, the librarians set out to reveal what information literacy concepts were being taught in which classes. The intention was to ensure that students were exposed to all of the five ACRL information literacy standards during their two-year careers at the institution. Librarians at Loyola Marymount University performed content analysis on syllabi across the curriculum, matching learning goals in the syllabi to information literacy skills in order to help departments identify individual courses that met institutional information literacy goals.[41] Librarians at Cornell University mapped the library's instruction records against the institutional curriculum to better understand how their efforts and staff allocations related to the larger curricular picture at their institution.[42] There are many case studies of curriculum mapping of information literacy in the LIS literature for librarians to draw from in designing their own local curriculum mapping initiatives.

Thinking about information literacy more broadly may also include hitching the library's goals to institutional goals for student learning.[43] Information literacy should be viewed as an institutional learning goal, just as writing, reading, and critical thinking skills already are. Librarians should advocate tirelessly for information literacy learning goals to be included in institutional strategic and assessment plans. A number of authors and presenters discuss having information literacy included in their institution's general education statements, including Oxford College, Seneca College, and the University of Arizona.[44] In fact, the University of Arizona requires information literacy in all proposals for new courses, and a librarian is included in the committee that reviews and approves such proposals. Again, this transfers some of the responsibility for teaching information literacy to teaching faculty while also helping teaching faculty reach their goals of increasing student learning.

In nearly every article examined in this section, the authors discuss how curriculum mapping increased conversations with teaching faculty. These conversations helped librarians deeply understand departmental and institutional curriculums and therefore target their instructional efforts more effectively and efficiently. Teaching faculty also came to understand what librarians do, which led to more effective and efficient collaborations. Above all, such conversations helped to make it apparent to everyone that both parties are working toward the same lifelong learning goals for their students.[45]

Question 4:
Lifelong Learning and Developing Complex Research Skills over Time Require Students to Transfer Their Information Literacy Skills from One Context to Another. How Do Librarians Teach for Knowledge Transfer?

One of the overarching goals of information literacy is the creation of lifelong learners, or as Morgan puts it, "enabling a kind of do-it-yourself (DIY) epistemological inquiry."[46] However, very little research has been done to determine if this actually happens. Scholars in the fields of rhetoric and composition have spent much effort examining how educators can promote transfer of writing skills from one context to another, which can help librarians think about information literacy transfer. Scholars such as Brent and Benander and Lightner stress that transfer is not automatic and that educators need to design instruction that promotes the likelihood of transfer.[47] The five broad ways that educators can encourage knowledge transfer among students in writing-from-sources assignments include developing metacognition, a toolbelt of literacy problem-solving strategies, generative dispositions, cueing, and providing varied opportunities for practice.

Metacognition is the most important activity for the promotion of knowledge transfer.[48] In fact, Lindenman writes, "Metacognition is almost universally lauded in composition studies as a key method for promoting successful transfer of learning."[49] If students consciously understand their thought processes when writing-from-sources, they are more likely to have control over these processes even in new contexts.[50] Pacello found that explicitly teaching metacognition in a developmental reading and writing course enabled students to transfer skills from his class to their other classes.[51] Educators can help students develop relevant metacognitive skills through structured low-stakes writing exercises that encourage students to reflect on writing-from-sources assignments before, during, and after the research process.

In addition to developing metacognitive skills, it is important for students to develop a "toolbelt" of problem-solving strategies from which they can draw when they encounter the numerous problems that occur during the research process.[52] Chapter 4 provided a numbered list of reading comprehension strategies, and chapter 5 provided four strategies for synthesizing information. Problem-solving strategies for writing are harder to put into list form, but they are described throughout this book. These problem-solving strategies, when combined with the metacognition to recognize when to use them and how to evaluate their effectiveness, enable and empower students to use what they already know to solve a variety of problems they will encounter in the future.

Dispositions also play an essential role in enabling knowledge transfer from one context to another. Dispositions are described by ACRL's *Framework* as "ways in which to address the affective, attitudinal, or valuing dimension of learning" and are built into each of the document's six frames. Driscoll and Wells looked at dispositions' effect on writing transfer and found that four generative dispositions (value, self-efficacy, attribution, and self-regulation) impacted whether or not students are able to transfer their knowledge. For example, if students felt the class or assignment was of value, they were more likely to be motivated to invest the cognitive and affective resources required for knowledge transfer. Driscoll and Wells conclude, "What these four dispositional theories and our participants show is that dispositions matter—generative dispositions, like a student's willingness to self-regulate or to positively value writing, will assist in their ability to transfer knowledge."[53] Educators should look for ways to create writing-from-sources assignments that promote generative dispositions such as curiosity and goal pursuit and reduce disruptive dispositions such as impulsiveness and distractibility.

One of the arguments for transitioning from "bibliographic instruction" to "information literacy instruction" was that students would be more likely to transfer skills and knowledge that are conceptual in nature. The literature on writing transfer agrees that generic knowledge and skills are indeed more likely to transfer than specific knowledge and skills.[54] However, students—particularly weaker students—will not always understand how to apply such generic knowledge or skills to a specific situation. Educators can use cueing techniques to gently remind students what they already know and "to help them make connections that might otherwise elude them."[55] Cueing techniques often come in the form of questions, such as those to promote reading comprehension presented in chapter 4. Cueing, along with other scaffolding techniques, should be gradually reduced over the learning process to encourage students to develop an independent ability to retrieve relevant background knowledge and skills to solve research problems.

The reading and writing skills described in this book are high-level skills, not ones that can be briefly described and then adequately understood and practiced. As has been seen throughout this book, scholars argue that reading and writing skills do not automatically transfer from one domain to another. Students need help transitioning their literacy skills to new disciplines or genres. When students are given varied opportunities to practice newly learned literacy skills, they develop their toolbelt of problem-solving skills and increase their sense of self-efficacy, as a personal history of success is likely to fuel their confidence and motivation to succeed in the future.

Question 5:
How Do Librarians Manage Change at the Program Level?

A full adoption of a situated and process-based view of information literacy requires academic librarians to seriously rethink information literacy instruction and perhaps even reference services on a programmatic level. I recently attended ACRL's Immersion Program, in the Program Track. One of the questions that we were asked in our preprogram assignment was whether our libraries had an instruction *program* or a conglomerate of separate activities. Nearly every Immersion participant I talked to felt they did not have a cohesive program; rather, individual librarians had their own initiatives with very little connection between each other. While individual librarians and teaching faculty can collaborate to make meaningful changes to their students' learning experience in regard to supporting process-based writing-from-sources assignments, the most significant changes will happen at the level of an information literacy program.

Establishing a programmatic commitment to process-based information literacy situated within reading and writing will require a major change in thinking about the research paper assignment. Such large changes should be managed carefully. Kotter, a retired Harvard Business School professor, wrote some highly influential texts on change management.[56] In these texts, he established eight necessary steps to any institutional change:

1. Establishing a sense of urgency
2. Creating the guiding coalition
3. Developing a vision and strategy
4. Communicating the change vision
5. Empowering employees for broad-based action
6. Generating short-term wins
7. Consolidating gains and producing more change
8. Anchoring new approaches in the culture

Kotter writes, "No matter how capable or dedicated the staff head, guiding coalitions without strong line leadership never seem to achieve the power that is required to overcome what are often massive sources of inertia."[57] He says that the leaders of change—who do not have to be top managers—must develop a sense of urgency and maintain motivation to work toward the new vision until everyone in the company has thoroughly adopted the change, which can happen only over time.

While his work primarily analyzed for-profit corporations, it can easily be applied to any type of organization. In two recent *Reference Services Review* articles, Farkas and Carter describe how the eight steps of the change model could be or were used to develop a culture of assessment in academic libraries.[58] Both of these authors stress that change management using Kotter's model requires changing people's behaviors as well as their attitudes. Carter describes how the guiding coalition was successful in changing the behavior of librarians at Auburn University but was not sure if attitudes toward assessment had truly changed. She admitted it was still too early in the initiative to be able to adequately view the long-term effects of the change.

Learning in groups is an important aspect of constructivist learning and applies to educators as much as it applies to students. Interactions with colleagues is one of the lenses through which Brookfield encourages educators to reflect.[59] The literature on communities of practice (CoPs) can assist instruction coordinators or library administrators on getting librarian buy-in and taking advantage of the collective expertise of the local library faculty in the transition process. Henrich and Attebury explain that "the key characteristics of communities of practice include a group, a common goal or interest, and a willingness to share and/or create knowledge in a safe environment."[60] CoPs are democratic and often informal, with facilitators rather than leaders. Librarians at the University of Idaho and Loyola University New Orleans benefited from flexible CoPs that balanced formal presentations with flexible time to share news and questions.[61] CoPs could be a powerful model to turn rhetoric and composition theory into improved information literacy instruction practice in a community of peers.

Instruction librarians are undergoing a profession-wide change as they grapple with interpreting, implementing, and assessing ACRL's *Framework*. As anticipated in a time of change, there is the expected resistance and healthy skepticism toward the *Framework*.[62] Moving toward a process-based and situated concept of information literacy is likely to provoke a similar reaction among instruction librarians. Both require a fundamental revision in how one understands and teaches information literacy. These two visions for change can be combined into one single vision. A rhetorical view of information literacy enhances one's understanding of the *Framework*, as has been demonstrated throughout this book. Librarians who become the local guiding coalition for change at their institutions should help their librarian colleagues develop a solid understanding not only of the *Framework*'s six frames, but also of the rhetorical and cognitive foundations of information literacy. This will help them create a vision that can be shared with others (both within and outside the library) in both short elevator speeches and also in more detail as needed to communicate with all interested parties across campus.

Conclusion

While schema theory, which was introduced in chapter 1 and elaborated on in chapter 4, stresses that schemata are flexible and can change, such change is usually small. The more developed a schema is, the more difficult it is to change in large ways. Thus it is very difficult to dramatically change an academic librarian's schema of information literacy. Yet reconsidering information literacy through the lens of rhetoric and composition theory has dramatically changed my own schema of information literacy. In fact, it has turned it completely upside down and inside out.

The problems with traditional approaches to information literacy are well documented and include a tendency to overemphasize search and retrieval, a lack of theoretical approach, artificial divisions between research and writing, limitations of the one-shot model of information literacy instruction, an unlikelihood of promoting knowledge transfer, and a misleading linear view of research. Holliday and Rogers warn that "narrow conceptions of [information literacy] can limit student learning."[63] I strongly suspect these same issues also lead to dissatisfaction and burnout among librarians.

A rhetorical approach to a process-based information literacy can greatly enrich the profession's understanding of what information literacy is and how to teach it. In such an approach, librarians acknowledge that "the writing and the research are inextricably intertwined."[64] Information literacy is situated between reading and writing, and any attempt to draw a distinction between them will be artificial and harmful to student learning. The messy and iterative inquiry process can be taught only through a process-based model of information literacy built on constructivist pedagogy. This will involve librarians expanding their knowledge into areas of the research process they have previously taken little responsibility for while also letting go of control in other areas.

Such an approach dramatically changes the perceived purpose of a research assignment for students as well as their educators. Hillard encourages readers to think "of the library not as some vast storehouse of data, but rather as an elaborate house of argument, a site where users activate and reactivate conversations and disagreements across time and space."[65] Writing-from-sources is not about finding an answer, but constructing one.[66] Holliday and Rogers say librarians should help shift the conversation away from "finding sources" to "learning about" topics within a discipline.[67]

Even how educators think (and teach students to think) about information sources will change. Instead of focusing on superficial indicators of quality, students will be taught that sources represent people and their worldviews.[68] Students would come to see that sources "are people with ideas who are developing those ideas over time and within a community."[69] This requires helping students to truly understand the information sources they are being asked to read. Only then will they be able to not only engage in the retelling of the knowledge accumulated by others, but actually *respond* to the authors of their sources as they transform their own knowledge.

Over the past few decades, librarians have shared many characteristics and goals with professionals concerned with Writing across the Curriculum, but a shared theory has been left wanting.[70] Elmborg argues that if librarians were to join the Writing across the Curriculum movement with a shared theory, a "more powerful, more dynamic, and more effective instructional practice can be achieved than either has been able to achieve alone."[71] But in order to achieve this, all stakeholders must share a common "vision of what becomes possible through their work."[72] If librarians were to develop a thorough understanding of composition and rhetoric *as it relates to information literacy*, they would be able to help bridge the artificial divide between research and writing, improving direct instruction with students and indirect instruction through advocacy with teaching faculty and other institutional stakeholders.

Like many other instruction librarians, I will continue to teach information literacy primarily in one-shot sessions with limited resources. Yet embracing this process-based theory and incorporating it into librarianship can make a difference in what our students take away from the library classroom. Burkholder, Fister, and Holliday and Rogers all conclude that how we talk about information literacy and writing-from-sources assignments matters to student learning.[73] Holliday and Rogers write, "We must be more intentional about what we spend time actually doing with students in the classroom, the library, and in online instructional spaces."[74] I do not pretend that such an approach to information literacy will be easy, but it will be more authentic and lead to greatly increased opportunities for knowledge transformation among our students.

Notes

1. James K. Elmborg, "Libraries and Writing Centers in Collaboration: A Basis in Theory," in *Centers for Learning: Writing Centers and Libraries in Collaboration*, ed. James K. Elmborg and Sheril Hook (Chicago: Association of College and Research Libraries, 2005), 9.

2. Ibid.

3. Stephen Brookfield, *Becoming a Critically Reflective Teacher* (San Francisco: Jossey-Bass, 1995).

4. Ibid., 50.

5. Gary R. Hafer, *Embracing Writing: Ways to Teach Reluctant Writers in Any College Course* (San Francisco: Jossey-Bass, 2014); Peter Elbow, *Everyone Can Write: Essays toward a Hopeful Theory of Writing and Teaching Writing* (New York: Oxford Uni-

versity Press, 2000); Ruth Schoenbach, Cynthia Greenleaf, Christine Cziko, and Lori Hurwitz, *Reading for Understanding: A Guide to Improving Reading in Middle and High School Classrooms* (San Francisco: Jossey-Bass Publishers, 1999).

6. Lili Luo, "Fusing Research into Practice: The Role of Research Methods Education," *Library and Information Science Research* 33, no. 3 (2011): 191–201; Marie R. Kennedy and Kristine R. Brancolini, "Academic Librarian Research: A Survey of Attitudes, Involvement, and Perceived Capabilities," *College and Research Libraries* 73, no. 5 (2012): 431–48.

7. Jeremy McGinniss in discussion with the author, August 2015; Joseph Bizup, "BEAM: A Rhetorical Vocabulary for Teaching Research-Based Writing," *Rhetoric Review* 27, no. 1 (2008): 72–86.

8. Donna Witek, e-mail message to author, October 6, 2015.

9. Rebecca Summary and Eleanor G. Henry, "Opportunity Cost," in *Encyclopedia of Business Ethics and Society*, ed. Robert W. Kolb, vol. 4 (Thousand Oaks, CA: SAGE Publications, 2008), 1544–46.

10. Mary Evangeliste and Katherine Furlong, eds., *Letting Go of Legacy Services: Library Case Studies* (Chicago: ALA Editions, 2015).

11. Mary Evangeliste and Katherine Furlong, "Introduction," in *Letting Go of Legacy Services: Library Case Studies* (Chicago: ALA Editions, 2014), x.

12. Ibid., xii.

13. Megan Oakleaf, Michelle Millet, Liz Mengel, Amanda Albert, Erin Eldermire, and Jeremy Buhler, "Getting Started with Academic Library Value: Strategies for Initiating Conversations, Expanding Thinking, and Taking Action" (presentation, Association of College and Research Libraries Conference, Portland, OR, March 28, 2015).

14. Christine Pawley, "Information Literacy: A Contradictory Coupling," *Library Quarterly* 73, no 4 (2003): 424.

15. Susanna M. Cowan, "Information Literacy: The Battle We Won That We Lost?" *portal: Libraries and the Academy* 14, no. 1 (2014): 26.

16. Meredith Farkas, "How to Build a Sustainable Embedded Librarianship" (presentation, ALA TechSource Workshop, online, April 22, 2015).

17. Carrie Donovan, "Shaking Up the Sediment: Re-energizing Pedagogical Practice While Avoiding Bottle Shock" (slides from keynote speech at The Innovative Library Classroom 2015, Radford, VA, May 12, 2015), http://www.slideshare.net/TheILC/shake-up-the-sediment.

18. Elizabeth Dolinger and Meredith Farkas, "Leaving the One Shot Behind: Transitioning from Status Quo to Sustainable Integration" (presentation, Association of College and Research Libraries Conference, Portland, OR, March 26, 2015).

19. Ruth Colvin Clark and Richard E. Mayer, *E-learning and the Science of Instruction: Proven Guidelines for Consumers and Designers of Multimedia Learning* (San Francisco: Pfeiffer, 2011).

20. Joan R. Kaplowitz, "Creating the Online Learner-Centered Experience," in *Transforming Information Literacy Instruction Using Learner-Centered Teaching* (New York: Neal-Schuman, 2012), 149–77.

21. Gordon Muir and Holly Heller-Ross, "Is Embedded Librarianship Right for Your Institution?" *Public Services Quarterly* 6, no. 2–3 (2010): 92–109.

22. Katherine Stiwinter, "Using an Interactive Online Tutorial to Expand Library Instruction," *Internet Reference Services Quarterly* 18, no. 1 (2013): 15–41.

23. Melissa Bowles-Terry, Merinda Kaye Hensley, and Lisa Janicke Hinchliffe, "Best Practices for Online Video Tutorials in Academic Libraries," *Communications in Information Literacy* 4, no. 1 (2010): 17–28.

24. Kristina M. Appelt and Kimberly Pendell, "Assess and Invest: Faculty Feedback on Library Tutorials," *College and Research Libraries* 71, no. 3 (2010): 245–53.

25. Clark and Mayer, *E-Learning and the Science of Instruction*.

26. Stiwinter, "Using an Interactive Online Tutorial."

27. Annie Armstrong and Helen Georgas, "Using Interactive Technology to Teach Information Literacy Concepts to Undergraduate Students," *Reference Services Review* 34, no. 4 (2006): 491–97.

28. Farkas, "How to Build a Sustainable Embedded Librarianship."

29. Emily Daly, "Instruction Where and When Students Need It: Embedding Library Resources into Learning Management Systems," in *Embedded Librarians: Moving beyond One-Shot Instruction*, ed. Cassandra Kvenild and Kaijsa Calkins (Chicago: Association of College and Research Libraries, 2011), 79–91.

30. Farkas, "How to Build a Sustainable Embedded Librarianship."

31. Matthew Brower, "A Recent History of Embedded Librarianship: Collaboration and Partnership Building with Academics in Learning and Research Environments," in *Embedded Librarians: Moving beyond One-Shot Instruction*, ed. Cassandra Kvenild and Kaijsa Calkins (Chicago: Association of College and Research Libraries, 2011), 3–16.

32. Farkas, "How to Build a Sustainable Embedded Librarianship."

33. David Shumaker, *The Embedded Librarian: Innovative Strategies for Taking Knowledge Where It's Needed* (Medford, NJ: Information Today, 2012).

34. Char Booth, M. Sara Lowe, Natalie Tagge, and Sean M. Stone, "Degrees of Impact: Analyzing the Effects of Progressive Librarian Course Collaborations on Student Performance," *College and Research Libraries* 76, no. 5 (2015): 623–51.

35. Dennis Isbell and Dorothy Broaddus, "Teaching Writing and Research as Inseparable: A Faculty-Librarian Teaching Team," *Reference Services Review* 23, no. 4 (1995): 51–62.

36. Donna Witek, "Academic Librarians as Knowledge Creators," *Journal of Creative Library Practice* (December 5, 2014), http://creativelibrarypractice.org/2014/12/05/academic-librarians-as-knowledge-creators.

37. Farkas, "How to Build a Sustainable Embedded Librarianship."

38. A. Gabriela Castro Gessner and Erin Eldermire, "Laying the Groundwork for Information Literacy at a Research University," *Performance Measurement and Metrics* 16, no. 1 (2015): 4–17.

39. Julie Arensdorf, Heidi Pettitt, and Erin VanLaningham, "Community Gardening: Librarian-Faculty Instruction Partnerships to Cultivate Scholars across a Major" (presentation, Association of College and Research Libraries Conference, Portland, OR, March 26, 2015).

40. Mary Moser, Andrea Heisel, Nitya Jacob, and Kitty McNeill, "A More Perfect Union: Campus Collaborations for Curriculum Mapping Information Literacy Outcomes" (presentation, ACRL 2011, "A Declaration of Interdependence," in Philadelphia, PA, March 30–April 2, 2011), http://www.ala.org/acrl/sites/ala.org.acrl/files/content/conferences/confsandpreconfs/national/2011/papers/more_perfect_union.pdf.

41. Susan Gardner Archambault and Jennifer Masunaga, "Curriculum Mapping as a

Strategic Planning Tool," *Journal of Library Administration* 55, no. 6 (2015): 503–19.

42. Gessner and Eldermire, "Laying the Groundwork for Information Literacy."

43. Anne E. Zald and Michelle Millet, "Hitch Your Wagon to Institutional Goals," 2012, accessed August 15, 2016, http://digitalscholarship.unlv.edu/cgi/viewcontent.cgi?article=1144&context=lib_articles.

44. Moser et al., "A More Perfect Union"; Anne Barnhart, Ru Story-Huffman, Karla Fribley, Joy Muller, Brenna Helmstutler, and Yan He, "Faculty Are Lifelong Learners So Why Not Teach Them? Information Literacy Instruction Offered to Faculty" (presentation, Association of College and Research Libraries Conference, Portland, OR, March 28, 2015); Sheril J. Hook and Veronica Reyes-Escudero, "Librarians Influencing the Literature Core Curriculum," in *Teaching Literary Research: Challenges in a Changing Environment*, ed. Kathleen A. Johnson and Steven R. Harris (Chicago: Association of College and Research Libraries, 2009), 202–15.

45. Moser et al., "A More Perfect Union."

46. Patrick K. Morgan, "Information Literacy Learning as Epistemological Process," *Reference Services Review* 42, no. 3 (2014): 407.

47. Doug Brent, "Transfer, Transformation, and Rhetorical Knowledge: Insights from Transfer Theory," *Journal of Business and Technical Communication* 25, no. 4 (2011): 396–420; Ruth Benander and Robin Lightner, "Promoting Transfer of Learning: Connecting General Education Courses," *Journal of General Education* 53, no. 3 (2005): 199–207.

48. Elizabeth Wardle, "Understanding 'Transfer' from FYC: Preliminary Results of a Longitudinal Study," *WPA: Writing Program Administration—Journal of the Council of Writing Program Administrators* 31, no. 1/2 (2007): 65–85.

49. Heather Lindenman, "Inventing Metagenres: How Four College Seniors Connect Writing across Domains," *Composition Forum* 31 (Spring 2015), http://compositionforum.com/issue/31/inventing-metagenres.php.

50. Brent, "Transfer, Transformation, and Rhetorical Knowledge."

51. James Pacello, "Integrating Metacognition into a Developmental Reading and Writing Course to Promote Skill Transfer: An Examination of Student Perceptions and Experiences," *Journal of College Reading and Learning* 44, no. 2 (2014): 119–40.

52. Schoenbach et al., *Reading for Understanding*.

53. Dana Lynn Driscoll and Jennifer Wells, "Beyond Knowledge and Skills: Writing Transfer and the Role of Student Dispositions," *Composition Forum* 26 (Fall 2012), http://compositionforum.com/issue/26/beyond-knowledge-skills.php.

54. Brent, "Transfer, Transformation, and Rhetorical Knowledge."

55. Ibid., 416.

56. John P. Kotter, *Leading Change* (Boston: Harvard Business School Press, 1996); John P. Kotter, "Leading Change: Why Transformation Efforts Fail," *Harvard Business Review* 85, no. 1 (2007): 96–103.

57. Kotter, *Leading Change*, 7.

58. Toni M. Carter, "Assessment and Change Leadership in an Academic Library Department: A Case Study," *Reference Services Review* 42, no. 1 (2014): 148–64; Meredith Gorran Farkas, "Building and Sustaining a Culture of Assessment: Best Practices for Change Leadership," *Reference Services Review* 41, no. 1 (2013): 13–31.

59. Brookfield, *Becoming a Critically Reflective Teacher*.

60. Kristin J. Henrich and Ramirose Attebury, "Communities of Practice at an Academic

Library: A New Approach to Mentoring at the University of Idaho," *Journal of Academic Librarianship* 36, no. 2 (2010): 161.

61. Ibid.

62. Farkas, "Building and Sustaining a Culture of Assessment."

63. Wendy Holliday and Jim Rogers, "Talking about Information Literacy: The Mediating Role of Discourse in a College Writing Classroom," *portal: Libraries and the Academy* 13, no. 3 (2013): 258.

64. Wayne Bivens-Tatum, "Timing of the Research Question," *Academic Librarian: On Libraries, Rhetoric, Poetry, History, and Moral Philosophy* (blog), November 30, 2010, https://blogs.princeton.edu/librarian/2010/11/timing_of_the_research_question.

65. Van E. Hillard, "Information Literacy as Situated Literacy," in *Teaching Literary Research: Challenges in a Changing Environment*, ed. Kathleen A. Johnson and Steven R. Harris (Chicago: Association of College and Research Libraries, 2009), 16.

66. John C. Bean and Nalini Iyer, "'I Couldn't Find an Article That Answered My Question': Teaching the Construction of Meaning in Undergraduate Literary Research," in *Teaching Literary Research: Challenges in a Changing Environment*, ed. Kathleen A. Johnson and Steven R. Harris (Chicago: Association of College and Research Libraries, 2009), 22–40.

67. Holliday and Rogers, "Talking about Information Literacy."

68. Doug Brent, *Reading as Rhetorical Invention: Knowledge, Persuasion, and the Teaching of Research-Based Writing* (Urbana, IL: National Council of Teachers of English, 1992).

69. Barbara Fister, "The Social Life of Knowledge: Faculty Epistemologies," in *Not Just Where to Click: Teaching Students How to Think about Information*, ed. Troy A. Swanson and Heather Jagman (Chicago: Association of College and Research Libraries, 2014), 92.

70. James K. Elmborg, "Information Literacy and Writing across the Curriculum: Sharing the Vision," *Reference Services Review* 31, no. 1 (2003): 68–80.

71. Elmborg, "Libraries and Writing Centers in Collaboration," 1.

72. Ibid., 2.

73. Joel M. Burkholder, "Redefining Sources as Social Acts: Genre Theory in Information Literacy Instruction," *Library Philosophy and Practice* (October 2010), 1–11, http://digitalcommons.unl.edu/libphilprac/413; Barbara Fister, "Teaching the Rhetorical Dimensions of Research," *Research Strategies* 11, no. 4 (1993): 211–19; Holliday and Rogers, "Talking about Information Literacy."

74. Holliday and Rogers, "Talking about Information Literacy," 268.